Ann marie
HOUGHTAILING

How I Created A Dollar Out Of Thin Air

How one woman built a company with $5 and a
Mac Book in the worst economic climate of her life

Ann marie Houghtailing

ISBN: 0988618206
ISBN 13: 9780988618206

Library of Congress Control Number: 2013901373
The Houghtailing Group
Chula Vista, CA

Jacki
Live your
Decadent
Dream

For those who doubted me and those who never
had a doubt - I thank you for your contribution.
You served me in equal measure.

GET ACCESS TO
Exclusive Content!

For *"How I Created a Dollar Out of Thin Air"* book owners <u>only!</u>

Ann marie HOUGHTAILING

As a token of my appreciation for purchasing my book, visit the link below and get access to my VIP membership area where you'll get access to exclusive content.

Make sure you get access to my latest tools, tactics and strategies.

Get exclusive access to:

- training videos
- workbooks
- webinars
- and more...

To sign-up, go to www.AnnmarieHoughtailing.com/VIP

Acknowledgments

I would like to acknowledge my parents who raised a warrior instead of a princess and empowered me to claim my place in the world and never demanded I be anything other than myself. A special thank you to my mother for working so incredibly hard to support her family all on her own. She has helped me raise my sons and given me the space to build an incredible life – thank you Mom!

All of my work has been refined and expanded thanks to my dear, dear Marketing VP, Linh Tang who has never failed me, always championed me, and helped me to grow.

My life and work is deeply and profoundly enriched by the remarkable people I have the privilege to call my friends. I thank each and every one of you for being the family I chose and astonishing me with your incredible loyalty and love.

Thank you to my first readers, Carolyn Isaacs, Stephen Serieka, Susanne Romo, and Malia Holleron. I appreciate your time and contributions. I would also like to thank Ruthie Inacay for her citations, a job I dreaded and was so grateful to turn over to her capable hands. Thank you to Camille Quartz for transforming me into Rosie and making my vision a reality.

And finally a special thank you to my sons Jackson and Austin. You make me tea, make me laugh, and make me proud. I love you, I love you, I love you.

Introduction
Trailblazer

*"Do not go where the path may lead, go instead
where there is no path and leave a trail."*

RALPH WALDO EMERSON

When I was seven I wore skirts on my head. At the time I wanted
to be a nun and I loved going to confession, rosaries, and all the
accoutrements that went with being a nun. I even wore my skirt
when I was biking around on my pink Barbie bike or my Big
Wheels. My Big Wheels had a small plastic trunk to hold things
like rosary beads and holy water that I made myself - of course.
Being a nun turned out not to be right for me, at which point I
decided I would take over Shirley Temple's life singing songs and
wearing cute outfits. Off went my makeshift nun's habit. I made
my mother roll my hair in pink sponge curlers every night so that
I could replicate Miss Temple's lovely locks. Many precious hairs
were lost in a quest to achieve those perfect ringlets.

In many ways, at 43, I am only more of who I have always been.
I choose and design my life as it suits me. I was not designed to
punch a clock, or occupy a cubicle or office under artificial light.
My kind go crazy or whither to nothing under such conditions. My
people are those who create instead of wait and as Emily Dickinson
so eloquently said, "dwell in possibility."[1] I have nothing against
following a traditional path; in fact I think it's the right decision

---

1 Emily Dickenson, *The Complete Poems of Emily Dickenson.* (Boston: Harvard
University Press, 1999), 329

for many, if not most people. It's just not for me, and if it's not for you either, then you're reading the right book.

There is more than one way to live a life, and I believe that constructing a life of your own choosing is one of the single most powerful achievements you can accomplish. I have done outrageous and absurd things to earn a living over the course of my life, including but not limited to, working as a manager for a Rent a Center in Montana, dressing up in costumes for corporate events, and working at several jobs for bosses who were so angry at the world that I'm quite certain we could solve the world's energy crisis if we merely harnessed all that rage and converted it into energy. I had always suspected that getting paid to do what you love was not limited to a few extraordinary people; and I have always been more fascinated and enamored by those who live boldly and build something from nothing rather than those who remain firmly on the path.

The very wise, complicated, and sometimes controversial, Coco Chanel once said, "how many cares one loses when one decides not to be something, but to be someone."[2] Coco Chanel was a trailblazer by anyone's definition. She understood that once you commit yourself to the person you wish to be then everything superfluous falls away and a world of possibility breaks open and you are truly free.

I don't know this for certain, I don't have any empirical evidence or study to cite, but I think you ultimately make more money when you have fun and you're turned on by your work. Maybe it's because it doesn't seem like work so you work harder, which ultimately results in more money. Maybe I'm totally wrong, but I think that we only get one go at this life and a whole lot of it is spent earning money, so why wouldn't we want to enjoy our work?

While I have worked for organizations early in my career, I have always known that I was not built for cubicles, office politics, and arbitrary rules that favor conformity and control over productivity

---

2 Coco Chanel, "Quotes Coco Chanel", retrieved on December 31, 2012, http://www.goodreads.com/author/quotes/3004479.Coco_Chanel

and innovation. As a college student, I had always assumed that I would become a professor. I loved literature and writing. There was no better place on earth to me than academia. What could be better than lively dialogue, reading, learning, and teaching?

I was very lucky to have a mentor early in my academic career tell me that I should seek opportunity outside of university walls, because I would be bored and deeply dissatisfied by the politics and fear that seems to surround the pursuit of tenure. He was 100% correct, and I am very happy that I did not travel the path of an academic, instead blazing a trail of my choosing. It would have fit me about as well as Cinderella's slipper fit her evil stepsister's big, fat foot. I would have been uncomfortable and ill-suited for a realm that demanded I produce in a particular fashion and blindly conform to rules made by administrators.

Interestingly, I have found a way to create teaching opportunities and enjoy the pleasures of teaching without the stifling environment of academia. I have always made winding trails over and around well-worn paths. I suppose I prefer unchartered territory that might be rocky and uneven, but is decidedly more interesting and rich with potential.

After a brief stint on a traditional career path in the non-profit sector, I found real estate, and eventually an even better fit as a sales trainer. It's never been the excitement of a big transaction, but rather the relationships you develop with people. Even as I finish typing that last sentence, I know how very serious it sounds, but it's true. It's always been the people in my business that make my work meaningful and interesting, which is why I felt so lucky to find a job training people and working for a man who respected my renegade tendencies.

In January of 2009 I was working as a national sales trainer traveling the country making a very good living doing a job that I loved, and working for the best boss in the world. On what would be my last business trip I would take, as I waited for my luggage to come out of the carousel in my home airport of Lindbergh Field in San Diego, my boss informed me over the phone that our biggest client had cut their training budget, and as of immediately – my job was over. This is the kind of call that's a lot like getting a roundhouse kick to the stomach. A combination of disbelief, panic, and numbness conjoin to produce a wave of heart palpitations, dry mouth, knee weakness, and stomach pain.

Even though I had suspected that this would happen, nothing really prepares you for the moment that you're dispensed with and find yourself unemployed, uncertain, and terrified.

I could tell you that when I was laid off I skipped towards my bright, shiny future bursting with possibility with unflappable confidence and Zen-like peace; but in truth I was devastated and scared. I didn't have much money saved; I didn't have a husband or partner to help me along, or a family that could financially provide for me. In addition, I had two children and a mother to support.

For most of my career I've been a private contractor, which is a lot like being a cowboy. You get the job done with little to no supervision and you move on. It's quite different from being a paycheck collector and having to answer for your time, but even as a cowboy I wasn't really living my highest dream. Someone else was creating opportunity and I was supporting his or her work. It was a good way to earn a living for a while, but I wasn't realizing my full potential or stretching myself.

You may recall that January 2009 wasn't what one would call an optimal market to launch a business. The global economy was spiraling into an unknown fate and every prediction by every expert for the future was worst than the last. It was in this whirl of uncertainty that I set out to build what I affectionately refer to as my "empire" with a small 'e.' The only thing empire-like about my business at the moment, is that I have built it and run it myself. For me it is the quintessential expression of freedom and limitless possibility. I'm fairly certain that Oprah and Bill Gates won't be calling me anytime soon to barbeque and talk about the struggles of running an empire. Thus far I haven't even gotten a call from Forbes to tell you the truth, but I'm doing pretty well for a girl who started off with more anxiety than money to launch a business.

I began building with little more than the gracious support of my remarkable family and friends. I had a budget of zero dollars, infinite passion, boundless energy, and unabashed conviction with which to purchase both my business license and my future.

Being a single mother with two boys and a mother to support can be daunting. To make the decision to start a business in the worst economic climate of my lifetime against the backdrop of personal struggle wasn't without real consequences and some difficult moments, but I forged ahead and today I'm proud to report that it's the most important professional and personal decision I've made to date.

In just over a year from making that decision, I partnered with a private University to launch the Institute for Sales and Business Development, I created a young adult executive program called Blaze My Trail, I have grown my consulting practice, I have speaking engagements booked throughout the year, and I'm working on projects that feed both my soul and my stomach. Even as I write this book I'm living my dream to write and perform my one-woman show. My show has been performed in Santa Fe, New York, San Diego, San Francisco, Chicago, and will soon be going to Los Angeles.

Being able to create your own opportunity is more than a philosophy; it's a way of being and behaving in the world. To do this work, one must be highly adaptable, self-reliant and in charge of his or her future. You're happening to life - life is not happening to you. When I think of some of the great artists, business people, activists and game-changers of our time, I think of them as people who left a trail rather than followed a path. They didn't whine about their bad luck, they made their own luck in life. They didn't hope for good things to happen; they went out and made them happen.

I still work hard, but I work on my terms. I'm on a journey that requires a diet of patience, a word that doesn't leap to mind for those who know me well. This isn't a book about how to get rich quick or a gimmick to find your next job; this is about how to design a life of your choosing. This is about owning your potential for a joyous, prosperous life that reflects your passion.

Despite the modest nature of my empire, from the outside it appears that I took off like a rocket and I was practically tripping over opportunities in my path. Let me assure you I had no such rocket. In reality, I struggled mightily with working myself to death, being a patient mother in the face of enormous financial anxiety, sharp learning curves, and traveling steep peaks and desolate valleys at such a rapid speed that I could not acclimate fast enough; and sometimes lost my breath, and sometimes my footing. There were moments when I questioned my ability as well as my sanity. Now I know that I'll always be able to earn a living doing what I love; and I would make that journey all over again for that single piece of knowledge.

People who have either heard me speak, taken a class I taught, read an article I wrote, or simply found me through social media, reach out to me and want to know how I'm building my modest little empire. I don't have an MBA or PhD and I haven't written a book (except for this one), so what's my story? I've learned a few things along the way and I know what is required. This is what I know for certain:

You need tough innards. Tearing your own path in life is not for the weak of stomach or the weak of heart. You have to *believe* in your talent and be prepared to tell the world about it. This isn't an easy thing to do in the best of circumstances and gets considerably harder when you aren't sure if can both pay your mortgage *and* feed your children, but it's critical to know your worth and have the ability to express your value with elegance and grace, and without apology. Plenty of people will want to tell you why you can't. Tough innards help you to smile, nod, and prove them wrong. Oh, and thick skin doesn't hurt either. Think of something in a nice Teflon, or even better, bullet proof.

Don't wait for opportunity - create opportunity. My business is built on my ability to wake up and create something out of nothing. I can't wait for an inquiry to appear in my inbox, I have to ask for people to meet with me so that I can present them with mutually beneficial opportunities. Fortune favors the bold, so understand that creating opportunities requires a certain amount of courage and growing body parts you may not have previously possessed. You have to ask yourself and those you do business with to think in new ways, act with courage, and expand their vision.

Asking beats the hell out of wishing all day long. It's not good enough to be brilliant or talented or have the greatest idea in the world. You have to go out into the world and ASK for what you want. Being brilliant in your garage or your living room is unlikely to keep your lights on. The worst anyone can do to you is say no. Get comfortable with no. If two letters and one small syllable is the thing that's going to keep you from success, you have no business in the game. Go home and get yourself a regular job. You aren't going to be an entrepreneur, a rock star, or a talk show host; you won't travel to Italy for a year or start your own clothing line -thanks for playing.

Your attitude is your truth. Your attitude is not incidental; rather it's a critical component of your success. Henry Ford said, "Whether you tell me you can or you tell me you can't, you're right."[3] I know that this is indeed true. Once someone lists all the reasons they can't do something, I know that they're 100% correct. Nothing I tell them or teach them will alter that truth, because they've deemed it so. Attitude is a decision. It is, as Viktor Frankl suggested, "the last of human freedoms." You choose your attitude, so select wisely and choose an attitude that expands rather than limits possibility.

We all need a small and mighty group. Surround yourself with people who believe in you and support your talent. If you look up and see petty, jealous behavior – you're not among your people. Move on. I don't know why people feel an allegiance to abusive, unsupportive people. I don't care how long you know someone. If that individual isn't positively contributing to your life, or worse still, is trying to diminish you in any way, you need to release them

---

3 Henry Ford, "Henry Ford Quotes," Retrieved on November 23, 2012, http://www.goodreads.com/author/quotes/203714.Henry_Ford

and make room for more worthy people. I don't possess some misguided sense of loyalty or romantic notion of love or friendship. If you truly love me and support me your actions will reflect your language. End of story.

Change never changes. The good and bad news about life is that it's always changing. When things are difficult we welcome change that moves us from pain and struggle on to higher ground, but when things are good we also have to remember that this too will change – eventually. Accepting this obvious fact of existence reminds us to savor the delicious moments and ride out the difficult moments.

Perspective. If you want to maintain a healthy perspective and manage your life here are some very simple rules:

- Don't be a victim. Remove all the excuses in your life and take responsibility for where you are in life.
- Never ask, "why me?" Instead ask, "What next?" Changing these two words can change your life.
- Don't blame people for your circumstances.
- Understand that nothing stays the same. You will not be in crisis forever. Evaluate a problem by asking if the challenge in front of you will matter in an hour, in a day, in a month, or a year? Most things won't.

Live your decadent dream. Designing your own life is really about identifying, articulating and living your decadent dream. Choosing to live your decadent dream is an act of courage. It is a decision, not an act of divinity or good fortune. Your decadent dream is living life on your own terms both personally and professionally.

Trust your talent and reach. I heard someone once say that his success was born from every opportunity that he had to grow into. If you set low expectations for yourself don't be at all surprised when you reach them. While I believe that it's critical to be able to deliver what you promise and more, I think that if you're always waiting to be smarter, more experienced or more confident, you might as well be waiting for Santa or the muse to show up. I prefer to create instead of wait. Everyone from T.S. Eliot to Dr. Seuss has warned against the danger of the waiting place where nothing ever happens. So don't ever wait.

Success is not an act of divinity. Success is designed. I think a positive attitude is important. Your attitude is your truth. If you think that you can make something happen, then you can. If you think it's impossible, then you're right about that too. However, a positive attitude and imagining success is not going to get you very far unless you actually *act*. I can promise you that you will get nothing from doing nothing. Building an empire of any size requires committing yourself to a diet of daily scheduled activity. Dreaming is good, but doing makes it happen.

Accept your failure with grace and take criticism like the gift it truly is. Failure will always find time to humble you and there's no avoiding that, *but* you get to decide your relationship with failure. I recommend humor. I'm fairly convinced that without a sense of humor I would be a shell of a woman fighting off suicidal tendencies from dusk till dawn. Humor is a tool of resilience, which is by far the most important power tool you'll ever own. Resilience gets through the toughest matter and ensures that you show up the next day; and criticism is a gem that tends to be covered in a lot of hard edged, really ugly rock that can cut you and hurt, but underneath that rock is something pretty brilliant that can serve you in ways you never imagined. Both the good and the bad news about failure and criticism is that neither one ever kills you.

It's okay to cry. It really is okay to cry, but not in front of people, well your friends maybe, but not potential clients or colleagues. I'm not by nature much of a crier. Anyone who knows me well will tell you that I don't cry easily, but I've cried in the midst of building my empire. I've cried over everything from computer difficulties to my sons' inexplicable inability to remember to pick up their wet towels. I thought I was going crazy until a friend kindly reminded me that I was building an empire and she was pretty sure that people always shed tears in the midst of such activity. I don't cry much anymore, but when I do, I give myself a break. Kindness is something I've always willingly extended to strangers, but too often was stingy about dispensing to myself, but I've learned that generosity begins at home.

Celebrate along the way. I haven't always been good at celebrating along the way. You have this vision that your empire will be built and *then* you'll have a big event to celebrate all of your hard work and success. In truth you should celebrate the small wins as you get them. Truly, sometimes it's just getting the meeting that was an impressive feat all of its own. Savor your small victories because collectively they're an impressive accomplishment. Buy some ridiculously expensive tea, go to the beach and run in the ocean if you're fortunate enough to live near one, or have your friends over for dinner. Just take a moment to inhale and taste and feel the joy of modest victory.

You are your own boss so be the sort of boss you deserve. Be hard on yourself and demand a lot of yourself, but give yourself a break too. Be kind to yourself and reward yourself for all that you do. If you're going to work yourself to death, you might as well go and work for someone else. Working for yourself should earn you freedom.

Be tenacious and patient. Creating something from nothing is a lot of work, energy, and belief; and sometimes it looks like the landscape isn't changing. Be patient. Things don't grow before your very eyes. They take time, but if you keep showing up, and keep working, eventually things start sprouting all around you.

My empire with a small 'e' has scared the hell out of me, made me cry and made me wait, but it's all mine and worth every hard won lesson. Outside of my children, my empire has given me the greatest joy. There's no magical, perfect time to start a business, write your novel, open a café, or live in Paris for a year. It's all there waiting for you the moment you are ready to show up.

When I was in college I went bungee jumping off of a train bridge. The guy running the jump put my gear on and said, "We're going to count back from three. When we get to 1 *jump*, put your arms out, and fly. Living your decadent dream is a lot like that. You start with tough innards and a strong will, and you open your eyes and jump. Keep your eyes open, because you don't want to miss a single thing.

CHAPTER ONE

Tough Innards, Thick Skin, and Growing New Body Parts

"A person will sometimes devote all his life to the development of one part of his body - the wishbone."

ROBERT FROST

Our culture is full of books on getting rich quick, visualizing your success, and the easy way to everything, While I truly believe that people can create a life of their choosing, I'm here to tell you that it requires and demands courage and mental toughness. If it were easy - then everyone would be working doing what he or she loved and getting paid his or her worth. So you have to decide if you have what it takes to live your decadent dream and build your empire.

If you want to move to the countryside and make your living from bee keeping and making scrap metal sculpture, let me tell you a few things. A lot of people will think you're crazy. You better have tough skin and be able to manage the criticism,

1

questions, and snickering when you make the announcement that you're redesigning your life. When your first batch of bees dies from a rare virus and your mother is the only person who has purchased your scrap metal sculpture in the last nine months, you better have tough innards to keep you from eating rat poison and enjoying a little Drano chaser. But if you've grown the necessary body parts and are brave enough to take criticism you can do what seems like the impossible. If you hustle (because you WILL have to sell your honey and sculptures), then you will reap the rewards of being that rare person from your high school or college reunion who truly loves their life and earns money doing what you love.

I meet people all of the time who don't want their ideas challenged and who shut down when anyone offers them the slightest bit of criticism. I spoke to a woman who told me she felt like her family shouldn't ask her questions or challenge the validity of her business idea or question her in any way. She felt it wasn't supportive. This is complete rubbish. Every idea is not golden, every person is not going to be able to execute their dream life - you had better be prepared to address real obstacles if you want to achieve your ideal life. The people who challenge you are forcing you to analyze the veracity of your ideas. This is a good thing if their intent is pure. You need to be critical about your strategy. If you're building a house you need to know that its design and construction are sound. A dream is no different.

Let's use me as a case study. I'm 43 and 5'4 with an average body- type, okay I could lose 20 pounds. If I said I really want to be a Victoria Secret model, it would be reasonable that someone might ask me how I was planning to go about that.

I did not get to where I am by being precious about my feelings. Even though I certainly have feelings just like everyone else, I know that I need to be more committed to the outcome or final product than the fragility of my ego. We're all a little fragile and precious, but if this rules you then it limits you, and you ultimately won't be able to get what you want.

I've spoken with people who wanted to be writers, but were terrified to show anyone their work and became devastated by criticism. You have to have readers to be a writer. You need input and must be able to hear quality criticism. The best writing is created through rewriting.

I've also met people who will tell me that they met someone who didn't like their website or told them they would have a hard time selling their product, and these comments derailed them and caused them to quit. You can't make money or live your dream if you give up when you're challenged. You have to see challenges and struggles as opportunities in disguise.

Trailblazers are by nature bold, and being bold means that you're highly visible and vulnerable to the slings and arrows of those who have never done what you do, but have a strong opinion about how you should go about it. You're wearing a target that invites people to vocalize their positions. Some of their views and contributions will be valid, even valuable, and some will be completely, utterly useless and have no purpose other than to make you feel badly. Learn to hear things with more analytic consideration and less emotional reactivity. It's a skill that will serve you well.

Adversity and failure are part of the journey. Paypal, that now serves nearly 60 million users, was the fifth business started by its co-founder, and suffered enormous, epic challenges in its early years as told by the book, *Paypal Wars*. Oprah Winfrey talks about having her credit card cut up in front of her by a grocery store clerk who told her to put her food back. She didn't start out as a powerful, mega wealthy media mogul. Along the way, these people struggled. It's part of your story and your education; and when you see those moments through that lens you are better able to appreciate that these struggles are valuable.

I watched a documentary called *Born Rich* in which wealthy heirs talk about all of the money that they will or have inherited. In the film, Ivanka Trump recounts being ten years old outside of Trump Tower and her father telling her that the homeless guy on the street was richer than he was, because at the time The Donald was something like $8 million in debt. I wouldn't be so presumptuous to guess what Trump was thinking or feeling at that particular time, but if I were a betting woman I would bet that it didn't occur to him to quit or assume that this was the end of his empire. Struggle is either a motivator or an excuse. You get to choose which it will be for you.

Most business people I know have found themselves in debt, on the verge of losing their business, rebuilding a business or starting over at one time or another. It's simply a fact of functioning in the market, which ebbs and flows.

In an op-ed piece in the New York Times in 2009, Joanne Lipman talked about being willing to take risks and manage failure with a sense of humor. Lipman identifies Martha Stewart as the expression of this advice; "My favorite Christmas card ever came from Martha Stewart — while she was in prison in West Virginia. It was beautiful, on heavy paper stock, and showed a gorgeous wreath. And on the inside, homey as could be, it was engraved with holiday wishes from "Martha Stewart, Alderson, West Virginia." [4] As we all know Stewart emerged from the experience even more successful than she had been before her incarceration. She certainly had enough money to go and buy an island and never have to show her face again, but instead she came out of prison wearing a poncho her fellow inmates had knitted for her waving to cameras as if to say, "I'm back!" Martha's public failure and punishment was a motivator, not an excuse to pack up and retreat. You can dislike any of these people if you want, but you cannot disregard or diminish their tenacity and resilience.

Before you decide that you want to build your empire and live your dream, ask yourself if you're truly emotionally prepared to step off the path and negotiate unknown terrain. There will be moments of discomfort, hurt feelings, bruised egos and public failure, but wait, wait, wait! Before you toss this book in the trash and cuff yourself to a desk at a job that makes you want to cry, let

---

4 Joanne Lipman, "The Mismeasure of Woman," *New York Times*, October 23, 2009, A21

me assure you that you can learn to toughen up and once you start forging your own particular trail that's uniquely yours, you'll be empowered in ways you cannot imagine.

I consulted with one client who would abuse herself mercilessly after a failure and sink into despair over her every misstep. It was destructive and painful for her. We worked out a plan to evaluate her performance with a client, learn from her errors, and use that intelligence for future business. The process was simple and by using failure as a learning tool we lowered her anxiety and put her in a more empowered position.

The point is you can learn to manage your reactivity and be more productive, engaged, and happy! It's simply a decision to reframe your relationship with failure and alter your perspective.

We all try to mitigate our failures. I don't suggest that failure shouldn't bother you, but rather that you can find ways to leverage failure to serve you for future success. I talk about this with my children as well as with my clients, and I try hard to do this myself. If I can examine rather than internalize my disappointment, I can create enough distance so that I'm learning rather than pitying myself.

CHAPTER TWO

Create Instead of Wait
Don't Get Stuck in the Waiting Place

*"Don't be afraid of your fears. They're not there to scare you.
They're there to let you know that something is worth it."*

C. JoyBell

In "Oh the Places You'll Go," Dr. Seuss wrote, "The Waiting Place…for people just waiting. Waiting for a train to go or a bus to come, or a plane to go or the mail to come, or the rain to go or the phone to ring, or the snow to snow or waiting around for a Yes or No or waiting for their hair to grow. Everyone is just waiting."[5]

I've spent my entire life writing. Since I was old enough to hold a pen, I've made sentences and paragraphs and stories, and yet I had never called myself a writer until I had reached my very late thirties. I would tell people, "I write, but I'm not a Writer." I

---

5 Theodor Seuss Geisel, *Oh the Places You'll Go* (New York: Random House, 1990), 24

was waiting to be published and when I got published in a small literary press, I was waiting to be published in something bigger or better. And so I waited some more. I got a few articles published, but they too seemed meager, and so still I was not yet a writer and so I waited. And then I met Marni, who was like my Glinda from the Wizard of Oz. Do you remember what Glinda told Dorothy? She told her that the power was inside of her all along.

Dorothy's lesson is that everything is within her and right before her very eyes. Marni helped me realize I have always been a writer. I had been stuck in the Waiting Place, and like Dorothy I needed to go on my own journey to find what was in front of me and inside of me all along. When the Scarecrow asks Glinda why she didn't tell Dorothy before, Glinda says, "Because she had to learn the lesson for herself."[6] I'm a writer and have been a writer my entire life and will continue to be a writer until my last breath.

There's something dark and agonizing about the Waiting Place and I don't think it's accidental that Dr. Seuss places this in the middle of the book. The Waiting Place is where people are stuck in fear, where passions are stifled in paralysis, and dreams grow decrepit with age. I meet people who are waiting to go back to school, waiting to lose weight, waiting to make more money, waiting for the right relationship, waiting to get out of the wrong relationship, waiting for the right moment to live their lives. What are *you* waiting for? What ever that thing is, I can promise you that its arrival is not what is required to live a life of your choosing.

There's never a "good time" to pursue your decadent dream. If we all waited until we had enough money saved, were the right weight, and our lives were in a state of perfect harmony, we would never leave the safety of the path.

If you want to be a writer, you'll find time to write. It may be for 15 minutes in the morning and 30 minutes in the evening, but you'll do it. You really can have whatever you want in life if you give

---

6 Tim Dirks, "The Filmsite Movie Review of the Wizard of Oz," Retrieved December 31, 2012, AMC Filmsite, http://www.filmsite.org/wiza5.html

yourself the time and permission. You have to choose this moment right now in your life to do what gives you joy.

Choosing to live on your own terms is an act of courage. Think of Chris Gardner in the *Pursuit of Happyness*, the true story of a single father who was rendered homeless and became a stockbroker against all odds. When you think that you aren't in the right time of your life to blaze your own trail, rent that movie and ask yourself - what would have become of Chris Gardner and his son if he had taken a low paying job and waited for things to get better before he pursued grander opportunities?

I'm sure there are times in people's lives when they really can't move forward or create meaningful change for themselves, because tragedy or circumstance impedes their journey, but I think that more often than not people get stuck waiting.

I'm fairly certain no one looks back on their life and thinks, "I wish we would have never taken that vacation to Paris, and I really wish I had never learned how to speak Japanese, and I would do anything to take back that novel I published!" We tend to regret what we didn't say, didn't try, and how we wasted opportunity and time on things that in retrospect seem so small. Do you use language like, "This is not the right time?" or "I wish I could do that, or it would be great to be able to, (fill in the blank)?" If you use this construction, you're excising your agency and are very likely in a passive mode of operation.

Reframing your language can actually alter the way you think and consequently the way you behave. This sounds pretty squishy for a chick who's all about action and analysis, but I've observed a correlation with the way people speak, think, and behave. By the way, I include myself in this category "people." In the moments when I'm least engaged and in charge of my destiny, I sound like a fragile whiner. When I change my language and my thinking, I can have an impact on outcomes and get closer to my desired result.

My heart always aches a little bit when someone approaches me after a speaking engagement and says, "I always wanted to ...

(fill in the blank)." When I ask why they didn't (fill in the blank), they tell me that they were raising a family or working on their career, as if those things completely barred them from pursuing their passion. J.K. Rowling was a single mother on public assistance when she wrote *Harry Potter*, the most successful children's literary franchises in the world. John Grisham was an attorney when he decided being an attorney made him miserable and he wanted to be a writer instead.

When I ask someone why they don't start doing what they want to do now, they tend to shrug their shoulders, unable to articulate or understand that they are free to leave the Waiting Place whenever they choose. They just need to move their feet.

Being an agent of your success and happiness means you'll find ways to pursue your passion now. I'm not advocating quitting your job as a CPA and driving across the country in a van earning your living by making balloon animals along the way, unless of course that's been your life-long dream and you're willing to give up all of the security you have accumulated. In which case, I say do it, do it now. The decision to create your own opportunities has to be just that – a decision.

For every program I develop or project I pursue I advocate a philosophy of creating instead of waiting. My dream job was to teach, write, and speak while earning a good living that allowed me to travel, spend time with my children, and make people's lives a little better. Oh, and I didn't want to have to answer to anyone for my time, and have the kind of flexibility that allowed me to work when and where I chose. Strangely enough, no such job was ever listed on Monster.com or Craigslist. I asked around and most people treated me as if I had asked them for a job as unicorn.

Realizing that no one was going to pay me to be a renegade, I started with approaching a private university about launching a Sales Institute. At first they humored me by allowing me to teach one class. It was a class that was not on their schedule, a class that I created. They didn't have any job posted, they didn't call me and they weren't even hiring. From there I convinced them that an institute dedicated to sales and business development would be a powerful contribution to the community and would be a unique offering for an academic institution. I didn't wait for a job opening, I didn't wait until I was in business for five years, had written a book, or got my MBA. I approached the university on the merit of my idea and my competence to execute my vision, and that was enough.

As I was launching the institute, I spoke around town for any group that would have me. If more than two people were gathering to meet about something, I was happy to show up with a Powerpoint presentation and speak. Now I'm paid to speak around the world. I could have waited my entire life for someone to give me a chance or to get lucky. Instead, I made my own luck and took my own chances.

Plenty of people said 'no' to me along the way. Most people said 'no' to me, and still do in fact, but my sales, theater, and writing background has trained me to treat 'no' as a very small word, with very little power that frequently means, not now. I've also been a writer and actress, both of which are filled with constant rejection. As an artist you basically put your work into the world where someone is certain to tell you why you should be waiting tables or delivering mail rather than hurting their ears and eyes with your astonishingly bad work.

Understand that waiting and patience are not the same thing. What Dr. Seuss and T.S. Eliot are referring to is paralysis that prevents growth and possibility. Patience is something you'll need in abundance. Patience for yourself and those around you will keep you from becoming anxious and allow you to appreciate that even when things are not progressing at the rate you would like, they are still moving forward.

As I mentioned, building an empire is not for the weak of stomach or the weak of heart, so what if you haven't yet found your inner warrior to go take on the world full tilt? I su small, but begin! If you want to lose 45 pounds and and it seems impossible, try giving up soda and v

11

the block. The idea is not to do everything right now; the idea is to start by doing something right now. If my basic math skills still serve me well, walking one mile is more than zero miles, taking one class is more than taking none, and saving twenty dollars is more than saving no dollars.

If you don't begin, you risk living the life of T.S. Eliot's J. Alfred Prufrock. [7]

And indeed there will be time
To wonder, "Do I dare?" and, "Do I dare?"
Time to turn back and descend the stair,
With a bald spot in the middle of my hair–
[They will say: "How his hair is growing thin!"]
My morning coat, my collar mounting firmly to the chin,
My necktie rich and modest, but asserted by a simple pin–
[They will say: "But how his arms and legs are thin!"]
Do I dare
Disturb the universe?
In a minute there is time
For decisions and revisions which a minute will reverse.

Eliot's decisions and revisions are the Waiting Place of Dr. Seuss. I challenge you to disturb the universe. I challenge you to *dare*. That's what it means to blaze a trail for yourself. It means you'll have to kick up some dust, and get dirty and that things won't often be neat and tidy. Living a life that you designed means that your closets might look a lot like the "before" picture from a Container Store ad, but sometimes you have to decide between color coordinating your towels or learning to Tango.

If you've ever said, "Someday I'll get to Egypt, the pyramids will always be there," or "Next summer I'll take surf lessons, the ocean isn't going anywhere," know that while that may be true, someday can be today. There will never be the perfect moment. By the time your kids are grown and you have enough money, you might have a bad hip.

Eliot, Thomas, "T.S. Eliot, Prufrock and Other Observations," Retrieved on ~mber 31, 2012, Bartleby.com, http://www.bartleby.com/198/1.html

Whether I'm conducting sales training or privately coaching people, I tell them that activity breeds results. You get nothing from doing nothing. Now let's be honest here, a lot of stuff looks like activity that's really just busy work and a distraction that keeps you from what really matters. Directed, meaningful activity is the vehicle you drive to get out of the Waiting Place. It's the thing that moves you. Commit to doing the hard work, even if it's in small doses, but commit.

Spend some time asking yourself questions and assessing your tolerance for commitment and risk and create a plan that's comfortable for *you*. I'm someone that can stomach risk and has a lot of confidence in my ability to create what I want, but you have to do what's right for you.

Ask yourself:

- Are you doing what you love?

- If there were no chance of failure, what would you attempt?

- What is your decadent dream that you quietly wish to yourself?

- What is the single biggest obstacle that you believe impedes your ability to blaze your own trail?

- What are you willing to do to overcome that obstacle?

- Are you willing to start *today*?

- What would you give up to live on your own terms?

- How important is it for you to be in charge of your success and your happiness?

- What variables are within YOUR control that you can change?

- What is it about creating your own opportunity that causes you the most fear or anxiety?

- How do you think your life would be different if you were doing what you loved?

These questions allow you to have a dialogue with yourself, and start creating instead of waiting. Once you have these answers you can develop an idea of what you want your life to look like and what you need to do to get there. In my experience, most people have never given themselves permission to think expansively about the life they really want; and for this reason never seriously consider what would be required to achieve that life. Until you've allowed yourself to consider what you want and how important it is to you, it's not possible to figure out how to get there.

Getting out of the Waiting Place also requires motivation. I can't count how many times I've been asked about the secret to sustaining motivation. It's the bane of the entrepreneur and business developer's existence. Motivation doesn't always meet you in the morning with your cup of coffee. Sometimes you have to go searching for it like a lost shoe or misplaced set of keys. We all struggle with locating motivation, but if you wait for the muse to show up – you're going to go hungry. Sometimes motivation is a raging fire that cannot be tempered, but more often than not it's a petulant, ill- behaved child that needs to be prodded and cajoled.

I'm extremely passionate and excited about my work, but even I have moments when I have to prod myself into action. High performers, and I'm sure even Olympic athletes, don't feel intensely motivated every day of their lives. So how do we manufacture motivation?

Don't wait for the muse to arrive. Waiting to feel creative or motivated is going to suck up a lot of time and puts you in a very passive, ineffectual position. Understand that you'll have to act even when you don't feel like it. Completely eliminate the notion and expectation that motivation will always come to you organically. Celebrate when it does and be prepared to manufacture it when it doesn't.

Calendar your action. If you book your activity like an appointment that you must keep, you're more likely to get things done.

Reward yourself. Sometimes when I'm writing or prospecting, I don't allow myself to get coffee until I've accomplished a certain goal or I'll reward myself with a mid-afternoon walk or a hot bath and a glass of wine in the evening. I'm my own boss, so if I don't embed rewards into my day, then no one else will.

Keep your eye on the prize. Remember what you're really trying to get. Beyond just the appointment, what do you want? A pied de terre in Paris, to pay off your bills, retire early, or take your family on an African safari? What ever it is, you need to remind yourself so that you don't get mired in tedium and forget your big vision.

Get over yourself. I know this sounds harsh, but when I'm feeling overwhelmed, I remind myself how damned good I have it and what a gift my life is, and it doesn't leave me much room to whine.

Remember that you have a choice. You don't have to do anything you don't want to – just keep in mind you aren't going to get what you want either. Motivation is a decision and while you can and should create external rewards to nurture your intrinsic drive, be aware that you choose to do what is necessary to get what you want – or you don't.

Create a space that inspires you. When my office is organized, I have fresh flowers on my desk, a pot of gorgeous tea and Vivaldi playing, I can work like a maniac. When I'm surrounded by noise, disarray and distraction, I have the focus of a gnat and the motivation of a sloth. Design a space that feeds your creativity and ignites your motivation.

Do things you find difficult first. I don't enjoy working out. I do it because I have to if I don't want to be a contestant on the Biggest Loser. I schedule time to work out early in my day so it's done and I don't have to think about it, otherwise I can forget going to hot yoga or Zumba at 7:30 at night. Although, you wouldn't catch me at hot yoga at any hour the truth be told.

Take care of yourself. Self-care is not necessarily a sexy topic, but if you're stuffing yourself with garbage, failing to get adequate sleep, and abusing your body in general, don't be surprised if your output reflects your input. This is an extremely challenging notion in a stressful culture that celebrates ease and rapidity over quality and peace. I struggle mightily with this myself, but we all need to understand that our bodies and minds are in fact our greatest assets and if we're careless we can pay a very high price.

Find your heroes and heroines. When I'm feeling like I want to just pitch a tent in funky town and take a nap, I think about all the people who I admire, from Coco Chanel to Joyce Carol Oates or a host of other people I perceive as having created their own lives, and it inspires me to rise above my petty slump. The last time I wanted to whine and drink wine, I thought: Martha Stewart would go clean a closet and then create a multi-billion dollar partnership after organizing her shoes. You can hate Martha if you want, but the woman epitomizes drive and motivation and just thinking about her shames me into action.

Do something instead of nothing. So often people don't want to work out so they'll do nothing and since they aren't doing anything, well they might as well eat a doughnut. Or since they don't want to prospect, they won't call anyone at all and just surf the Internet instead. It's better to make one call than no calls. It's better to write one paragraph than zero paragraphs and it's certainly superior to walk around the block than do nothing and devour a doughy, sugary, fat filled snack that will just leave you feeling bad about yourself.

When I was four my father took me to a pumpkin patch and told me that I could have *any* pumpkin that I wanted. Just as I had completed the film reel in my head of how I would become world famous as the owner of a pumpkin larger than Cinderella's carriage my father said, "So long as you can carry it." I pushed my disappointment into my lungs, took a deep breath, and found the largest pumpkin I could carry without crippling myself. My father wasn't raising a princess, he was raising a girl who would build her own muscles and grab her own desires. It took me a little while to appreciate that moment– about thirty years give or take, but I took the lesson to heart. Admittedly, I would never have executed the

16

lesson in quite this way with my own sons. I would say that there are gentler, tender ways to empower our children, but I do appreciate the message my father was trying to send. It's a powerful feeling to be able to get what you want all on your own at any age and every stage of life.

CHAPTER THREE

Ask Don't Wish

*"Asking is the beginning of receiving. Make sure you don't
go to the ocean with a teaspoon. At least take a bucket
so the kids won't laugh at you."*

JIM ROHN

As I referenced earlier, in my very late thirties I read an article in the NY Times that would forever alter the way I viewed the world and made me think hard about my life. The article was entitled *The Mismeasure of Women;* and suggested that the reason women don't get paid as much as men in great part is because quite simply, they don't ask. While the article highlighted how this specifically impacts women, it can apply to anyone who has wished instead of asked for what they want from life.

I've coached many executives who didn't get the raise, promotion, or opportunity they knew they deserved. They reach out to me to help them reposition their career and take greater control over their future. The very first thing I want to know is if they asked for the raise or promotion. Frequently, they respond by telling me how accomplished they are and how much more competent they are than their colleagues, but that isn't what I want to know.

Whether it's cultural, generational, or gender specific, there's a tendency for some of us to believe that if we just work harder than everyone else we will be rewarded. For some of us it may be part of a value system and set of beliefs rooted in the way we were raised. The problem with this belief is that it places far too much power in the hands of others. Wishing is like waiting. Why not ask?

We assume that success is a basic mathematic equation that goes something like: hard work plus competence equals success – and sometimes that's how it works except when it doesn't, which turns out to be more often than you imagine. People will say things like, "But I've worked hard, I shouldn't have to ask," or "I'm a good person, my time will come," or "If it's meant to be it will happen." With all due respect, I think that all of those responses are an excuse for being too scared to ask. I think that if you truly believe that success is not up to you and it's something to be gifted by someone more powerful than you, you have positioned yourself as a passive recipient rather than an active participant in life.

If the worst possible thing that can happen is that someone will say no to you then I say *ask*! Ask for business, ask for opportunity, ask for a date, ask to be treated differently, ask for consideration, and ask for anything and everything that will contribute to your well being personally and professionally.

Asking for what you want is not an expression of arrogance, but rather one of self-worth. I consider myself to be confident, and if you asked me in my twenties or thirties I would have certainly identified myself as having self-worth, but I had the sort of upbringing that in many ways trained me too well to be grateful for anything I got. It's important to be grateful, and I sincerely believe it contributes to the quality of your life; but if you are too grateful for *anything* at all, you may not feel entitled to much.

As I look back on my life, I recall many times that I accepted less and didn't dare to want or ask for more. Even simple things like accepting a meal at a restaurant that wasn't cooked to my liking. It was easier for me to just accept what was given to me rather than request what I really wanted. Somewhere along the way I got the notion that getting what I wanted was a special luxury and that asking inconvenienced others, which was bad manners. You can see how this sounds, well, crazy.

Asking is indeed an expression of entitlement, and while the very word entitlement has come to represent something quite negative, there is also a very positive connotation that is less frequently associated with the word. In point of fact, the word entitlement really means a deserved right. Therefore if you feel you have the right to something and you deserve it, you should ask for it. The operative word here is "deserve."

It's important to have earned some credibility and ask from a place of worthiness and decency. Asking should never be an expression of arrogance, but rather an action of self-advocacy rooted in credibility.

The famous millionaire Percy Ross once said, "You've got to ask! Asking is, in my opinion, the world's most powerful — and neglected — secret to success and happiness."[8] This is an intense statement about the power of asking and should inspire you to look carefully at what has kept you from having what you want. The answer might be – YOU.

Think about whether you ask for what you really want in restaurants, relationships, and at work. It's a great revelation that often, though not always, you can get exactly what you want simply by asking. There's no shame in wanting more from life and no nobility in passively accepting less.

There's an elegant and gracious way to ask for what you want. As I often remind my students, language can start wars, comfort

---

8 Percy Ross, "Percy Ross Quotes," Retrieved on November 23, 2012, Thinkexist. com, http://thinkexist.com/quotes/percy_ross/

the most anguished heart, and change the course of history. Never underestimate the power of language.

When you're making a request, particularly a considerable request, consider your choice of words and tone. It matters. You can be strong without being aggressive, polite without being apologetic, and confident without being arrogant. Asking is a bit of skill and a bit of art.

I like to take my sons to the swap meet. We enjoy old and interesting things as well as a good bargain. It's also a great place to teach my sons to negotiate and I rarely pass up real life opportunities to teach them how to blaze their own trail. On one particular trip my youngest son Austin, who was about twelve at the time, wanted a game for his game system. It was $20 and I told him to ask for a better price. That was all the direction I gave him.

When we walked up to the table he said, "Excuse me, this game is $20, I'd like it for $15, would that be alright?" The seller said, "I think that's fair." Austin thanked him and we walked away. While it's a lesson in negotiation, it's also a lesson in what you can get if you ask. Austin had five more dollars in his pocket, because he asked. Even at 12 you can teach your children to ask with elegance. I'm very proud of that moment because I know what it will mean for his life in a much larger context, and it isn't about bargaining, it's about possibility.

I have a program for kids called, *Blaze My Trail*. The program teaches kids all the critical core skills that academic institutions do not. On the second day of one of our programs a dollar fell out of my pocket and a student noticed and handed it back to me. He jokingly said, "Can I have it?" I said, "Sure." All the kids were stunned – you can buy a lot of impact with one dollar among middle and high school students. "You're really going to give him that dollar?" One kid asked. The kid I gave the dollar to was the most stunned of all. I told them that sometimes when you ask you get what you want and then another kid responded, "Well, can I have $20?" I told him, "No, because sometimes you don't." Regardless of the stakes, there is a powerful lesson imbedded in that moment. Asking might get you something and rejection won't kill you.

On June 14, 2011 I had the idea of launching a movement. I was inspired by COO of Facebook, Sheryl Sandberg's Barnard College commencement address. Sandberg spoke about how women haven't come nearly as far as we think. She challenged young graduates to lean into their profession, and take greater responsibility for their power. One month later I was leading a town hall meeting, blogging and had launched a website inviting 1 million women to commit to making 1 million of their very own dollars. The Millionaire Girls' Movement was built with nothing more than passion and a bit of money and some incredible support from my marketing and technical partner, Linh Tang.

I literally had three followers: me, Linh and his wife, when I started e-mailing powerful women like international designer, Zandra Rhodes, fitness guru Tamilee Webb, and weight loss pioneer and magnate, Jenny Craig. I e-mailed them with a brief note with the website asking if I could interview them. Every one of them said, yes. Full disclosure, I did have lunch with Jenny Craig several months earlier, but I wasn't sure she would care about what I was doing or bother to respond to my request. Every single one of those first three interviews couldn't have occurred without my asking.

All of them could have said no to me; others have, by the way – and so what? I've had the pleasure of speaking with remarkable women who have shared their wisdom and I've been able to make that content available to other women - all because I sent an e-mail into the ether, making a request. Pretty amazing, right?

If you're disappointed by all the help you don't get, all the money you don't make, and the life you don't have, consider the possibility that you have to ask for all of those things in order to get them.

I once did a workshop on keeping the passion alive in your marriage – somewhat ironic that I was approached on the subject being that I'm not a therapist and I'm not married. One of the things I spoke about in depth was asking. Husbands and wives complained about all the ways their needs weren't being met personally, domestically, and yes, even sexually. My first question was always the same, "Did you ask?" Inevitably, across the board, the answer was, no.

Many of us expect that our spouses, co-workers, friends and children should know what we need. This assumption won't get you what you want, but more seriously it's damaging to relationships. You are responsible for ensuring that your needs are met and that you're respected. No one can read your mind and we all have very different ideas of how love, respect, appreciation and caring are expressed.

Asking for what you want, need and deserve is a courageous act of self-love that requires you to take responsibility for your own happiness and success.

I have one very important caveat to asking. Be worthy of what you're asking for and don't ask for something you don't deserve. You are a brand and when you ask for the sake of asking and you haven't earned what you're requesting, you compromise the integrity of your brand. You're effectively not credible and you'll lose rather than gain opportunity.

I coach people to ask with something to offer. Relationships are reciprocal and we're all more inclined to invest in those who invest in us. Consider what you have to offer the person you're asking and why they should grant your request. Your contribution should be evident. The reason that so many powerful women say yes to me to be interviewed for the Millionaire Girls' Movement is that I fund the movement and offer the information to women for free with the goal of educating and elevating the financial status of women. My contribution may not benefit the women I'm asking, but benefits women at large. So consider how you frame your request and make it easy for someone to say yes to you.

Asking will also help you to change your attitude about the wicked 'S' word - selling. Most of us aren't particularly comfortable with asking for opportunity, advancement, more money, an appointment, a referral or someone's business. It seems like the sort of work relegated to aggressive sorts that one might associate with bulldogs, sharks, and other tenacious members of the animal kingdom known for their single mindedness. We would all much prefer to just express our talents, skills and brilliance without having to engage in the unsavory business of "selling" ourselves.

It seems unfair, outrageous and overwhelming that in addition to having a skill, service or talent we must also be required to peddle it like a street vendor hawking snake oil from a covered wagon. Not to worry, you can elect to take a much different approach to selling your service, one that is elegant, ethical, and serves the client.

Because of my training, it would be remiss of me not to support your revenue generation efforts with a bit of sales and business development intelligence. So here is what you need to know to change your relationship with selling and business development:

You're trying to serve your client by educating him or her to make the best buying decision. It's not coercion or manipulation. Sell as an advisor, consultant, advocate, educator and expert, and everyone wins.

Most likely the person you're selling to is selling something to someone else. This is what our economy is built upon and we all just need to accept that.

Being the best does not mean that you don't have to sell. We all know complete incompetent idiots in our own industries making truckloads of money, so being the best isn't a barrier, nor is it an e-ticket to success. You still have to convey your value.

Learn how to develop your business. Despite popular belief selling is not the domain of the extrovert. When you unlock the little mystery of selling, your life gets a whole hell of a lot easier.

Don't get caught up with rejection. It's really not you and if you let it bother you it will disturb your success and limit your earning power – we hate that. Rejection is never delightful, but that doesn't mean it needs to be soul crushing either. It's really not such a big deal, just move on.

Learn to be your own best advocate. That's right, you should claim your piece of the pie because you deserve it. Do this with elegance and craft your language deliberately, but don't allow someone else to take an opportunity from you because you're unwilling to express why you're the right decision, and if you can't do this for yourself, you most certainly cannot rely upon someone else to do this for you.

Find someone who develops business successfully and become his or her student. Yes, grasshopper you must find a master to show you the ways of success. Don't be embarrassed or limited in your thinking. They already have it figured out and can mitigate the learning curve.

If you think that you're just bad at selling, then you're right and nothing and no one will change your mind so go and do something else. I'm not being glib. Your attitude is your truth. Decide that while you might not be an expert, you can be, and then over time, you will be.

Take risks, because fortune favors the bold. I didn't get to where I am because I waited for someone to notice me. You get the big opportunities because you let everyone know that you're ready and able. Don't be shy. Throw your hat into the ring and ask for what you really want. Some people will say 'no,' but eventually someone will say, 'yes.'

Decide that you can have fun and make money. Look, there are days that I'm intensely irritated, but ultimately, I really love my work and I know that when people write me a check, they're doing a good thing for their business. They aren't doing me a favor, they're taking care of themselves and I'm helping them. You have to *know* that what you do or what you sell has value or you aren't going to sell much or have any fun.

I know, I know, you're smart and hard working and special and that should be enough, and it absolutely would be if there was little competition, but we live in a highly competitive market full of choices and it's our job to educate our clients and defend our worth.

I have navigated this process of engaging in meaningful work and monetizing my talents. I help my clients to create their own meaningful work and I want you to know that you can do it as well, but you have to replace your resistance with receptivity.

Create a list of all the things you deserve and have never asked for and make a decision to ask for the raise, the respect, the time and the opportunity. Ask for whatever it is you have silently waited to be awarded. Go ahead. I dare you!

CHAPTER FOUR

Your Attitude is Your Truth

"Everything can be taken from a man or a woman but one thing: the last of human freedoms to choose one's attitude in any given set of circumstances, to choose one's own way."

VIKTOR E. FRANKL

L ife will happen to you. We are all at the mercy of external circumstances beyond our control. We are vulnerable to job loss, illness, death, divorce, and inexplicable suffering that knows no bounds. There's little to nothing any of us can do to protect ourselves from suffering, but we have complete control over how we will respond and rebound from life's misfortunes. This sounds abysmal I know, but hang in there with me for just a moment. I believe that your attitude is your truth.

Your attitude informs outcomes, and creates the reality in which you live. There are some people who have decided that their upbringing or their bad luck cannot be overcome. They believe that others have had it better than they have, and if they had the same good fortune they would be more educated, happier or wealthier. This is not the attitude of someone who can create a dollar out of thin air. Those who create opportunity insist that obstacles are opportunities disguised.

I didn't grow up wealthy. I grew up quite poor in fact. I've certainly had my share of disadvantage and I could make a compelling case that life is unfair. It's not fair by the way. Bad things happen to remarkable people and sometimes the bad guy wins. So what? This is not a reason to pack up and give in.

Consider Warren Buffet who said," I always knew I was going to be rich. I don't think I ever doubted it for a minute."[9] Who would Warren Buffet be if he had gone through life believing that amassing wealth was relegated to a small, group of privileged individuals? His belief was his truth. He also happened to be brilliant and highly disciplined - belief is clearly not enough, but it's a critical component to success.

I don't think he's likely to have ever taped affirmations to his mirror to recite every morning. He's more of a solid, mid-western sort of guy, but positive thought transcends geography and spiritual paths. It's a philosophical basis for moving through the world. There's no telling who Buffet might have been had he not harnessed the power of his belief and followed his passion. With all of his talent, would Buffet have been able to be WARREN BUFFET without his certainty? I can't prove it, but my answer would be an emphatic, resounding no!

Think of an athlete trying to increase her speed. If she thinks that it's impossible, she's trying to defy reality. If she believes that it's possible then she can do it. Belief changes her reality. A profound belief in yourself will not eliminate failure, but it will enable you to manage failure and use it as fuel to power you to your destination.

We live in a time of constant change requiring the greatest capacity for flexibility and resilience, both of which are driven

9 Warren Buffet, "Warren Buffet Quotes," Retrieved on November 23, 2012, Refspace, http://refspace.com/quotes/Warren_Buffett/rich

by your attitude. Taking responsibility for your attitude and your happiness removes blame, resentment, and excuses. It's liberating and powerful to be in charge of your attitude and to understand that no one has power over you unless you willingly surrender it.

For me, resilience is critical. Resilience can be fed with a lot of humor. I couldn't live without humor. The ability to laugh or make people laugh in times of struggle or pain is a precious gift. I've raised my sons to understand that it's not failure or a misstep that defines you, but how you manage the very next moment because that's the piece you have the greatest control over.

My youngest son, Austin took riding lessons. He was a jumper and loved it. Jumping over things on a horse isn't a sport that one equates with safety. I worried about broken bones or worse, but this is who my son is, and I want to respect his passion and support what he loves. His trainer was a lovely English guy who regularly reminded me that Austin would fall off of a horse. He told me this every lesson to remind me that this is what this sport means, to fall, to get up, and do it again. On a beautiful day in August Austin was on a pony that jumped over a vertical jump, landed sharply and slammed his head down, sending Austin sailing over his head into the dirt with a thud. Before I could speak Austin shot up like a rocket and planted himself firmly back into the saddle. He got into the saddle so quickly, he had not even taken the reigns, which his trainer reminded him was critical, lest the horse go racing off.

I admit that there was a moment when I wanted to leave and sign him up for soccer or tennis or ballet. There's really nothing like seeing your child being thrown to the ground to make you reevaluate a sport. With my heart pounding in my chest, I confirmed that Austin was unharmed. I told him how proud I was of how he got up. Graeme, his trainer, was sure to tell him that serious riders always fall, but they always get right back on. This doesn't mean that you can't feel fear, anxiety, or disappointment. Anyone who has ever set out to do anything worth doing has felt a heap of complex feelings along the way. But it's how you behave with those feelings that determine your future and your truth.

When I'm coaching someone who is struggling with an error they made, I tell them my own story of getting back on the horse. I was teaching my very first sales training program in Indiana. It was a seven-hour program that I was conducting without a script, strictly from memorization. If you've ever taught or delivered a speech you can appreciate that seven hours is a behemoth expanse of time for one person to educate and entertain a group about anything.

I taught a class of around 30 individuals in the banking industry who sat at tables that formed a U-shape. I walked up and down the inside of the U while I lectured and worked hard to educate them and keep them laughing. About 30 minutes into my presentation, I took a step back and fell on my ass. It wasn't a gentle tumble, but rather a violent WWF slam to the ground minus the wrestler. I was shocked, humiliated, and could feel a wicked bruise instantly forming on my backside and an even bigger injury forming on my ego.

I propelled myself so quickly to a vertical, upright position that my students were unsure what to do and collectively sucked in their breath uncertain whether to laugh or administer first aid. Once on my feet, I continued to lecture as if nothing had happened. When I changed the slide, I turned around and said, "I'm a little like an Olympic Gold skater, I fall, get up, and do the triple toe loop," to which the class burst out laughing for a good five minutes. I could have stopped the class, taken a break and cried in the bathroom, but elected to laugh at the absurdity and continue.

After the class I called my boss John Gehegan, who wanted a full report of my performance, since it was my first effort. I told him the truth.

"Miss Houghtailing! How did it go?"

"Good. The conversion rates were great and the evaluations were fantastic."

"I'm not at all surprised. I knew you would be great."

"Mmmm, thank you. I also fell." I said this in a much smaller voice. I was more than willing to be honest, but saying it out loud did in fact make me go a little quiet.

"You what?"

"I fell down."

"On the ground?"

"Yes, the usual place people fall."

"Are you okay?" John asked, sincerely concerned.

"I'm fine, just humiliated."

John then proceeded to laugh for what seemed like twenty-five minutes, though I'm sure it was more like five.

"Ann marie, in twenty years I don't think anyone has ever fallen down giving a presentation."

"Really? Well, what can I say? I'm an over achiever, I did it the first time out of the gate."

Be kind to yourself when you fall literally and metaphorically. Your attitude determines how you approach obstacles and problems. Trailblazers have challenges and problems just like everyone else in life. There's no magic that can protect you from conflict, tragedy and misfortune. How do you behave when you don't get a promotion, lose your job, get a divorce, spring a leak in your roof, or break your leg? Who are you in crisis? Those living their decadent dream treat problems like puzzles to be solved. There's always a solution. There's always a choice about the outcome.

No trailblazer is a victim of circumstance. It's what you do with the things life throws at you. Do you take what appears to be a mess and tell yourself there's nothing worth having and starve yourself from opportunity or do you have a delicious meal and feast on your own creation? Think about who you want to be in the world. Are you a visionary who sees possibility everywhere, even in the ruins, or are you someone who can only see the ruins?

I'm not a spiritual leader, a therapist or an expert on the human condition. I'm just a businesswoman, a mother, a friend, an ex-wife, a teacher, a writer and maybe a few other things, but that's all, really. I can't avoid heartbreak, suffering, or disappointment, but I can develop strong innards and a solid backbone. I can remind myself that happiness is not a thing you find or purchase or stumble upon, but something you choose and create and nurture. When you make a decision about your attitude the world expands and you harness a unique personal power that gives you mobility because you're not paralyzed by fear, self-doubt, or potential failure.

CHAPTER FIVE

My Small and Mighty Group

"Relationships are all there is. Everything in the universe only exists because it is in relationship to everything else. Nothing exists in isolation. We have to stop pretending we are individuals that can go it alone."

MARGARET WHEATLEY

Building an empire can be a lonely road at times. Populate your life with people who will cheer you on, pick you up, kick your ass, love you at your worst, see you through and see you out. In my life, those people are my small and mighty group of friends and colleagues. I always say that you're born into a family, but your friends are the people you choose, so be decadent and choose the best.

If you have people in your life who doubt your ability, criticize your ideas and are threatened by your success, you need to reevaluate your relationship. There are plenty of people along the way who will be too happy to judge you and doubt you. You don't need friends who will do the same.

Gertrude Stein once said that every writer needs a 'yes.' She was referring to that affirming voice that believes in you unconditionally and has no doubt about your talent and place in the world. Writing is such a hard road, fraught with rejection, self-doubt and disappointment, that it is critical to have a voice absent of everything but complete certainty. If you're creating your own way in the world you need this voice to be your truth, but even big, brave souls are human and need the warmth of a roaring cheerleading section.

My friends have been significant contributors to my personal and professional success. They're the family I chose, my personal Advisory Board - my village, if you will. I would do anything for them because I could not do any of this without them.

I built my company during a very tumultuous period in my life, but as I mention in Chapter Two, if you're waiting for the perfect time to do something, the perfect time may never come. You may find yourself relegated to the Waiting Place. When I set out to build my company I was also managing a difficult personal period in my life, balancing single motherhood, and a host of other challenges.

There were moments when I felt as if it was all too big and maybe I should just get a job at Target, which by the way, probably would have been a real challenge with the unemployment rate rising to double digits. The idea of wearing a red polo shirt and working as a cashier surrounded by fabulous products was so seductive that I began to see Target as the happiest place on earth. In my lower moments I walked by the computer they have to apply for a job in the store, holding my dish soap and wondering if I should just sit down, fill out an application and be done with it.

My friends gently reminded me that such an existence would probably challenge my sanity. Other friends suggested less gently that I wouldn't last a week having to answer to someone; and that punching a clock might actually incite some latent violent tendency in me, causing me to punch someone in the snout. With my interests and the interests of my potential fellow Target co-workers in mind, I was convinced to stay focused and build my empire. My small and mighty group believed deeply in me when I was exhausted, fragile and uncertain, and had lost belief in my self.

There are moments when you're so deep into what you're building that it's hard to see what's right in front of you. My friends explained this to me when I was in the depths of exhaustion, living off of a diet of uncertainty and questioning my capacity to make good decisions. They told me that it was all coming together and I was the only one who couldn't see it. I couldn't see it because it was like I was in the center of one of those paintings of dots. I was in the dots and I didn't see what everyone who was standing back saw.

I had my first opportunity as a trainer before I had a business license, a website or a business card. The opportunity was enormous and I was consumed with building the proposal, so without question or a single pause my friend Nicole designed a business card and my friend Mishel ensured that I got a basic web presence up. These were enormous gifts that freed me from tedious concerns that were critical and necessary, but not where I wanted to place my focus. I didn't ask for these things, they were generously offered. They wanted the best for me.

Your friends are people who celebrate your success rather than envy it as if it's a personal affront. I want my friends to be healthy, happy, in love with the right person, building families and careers and living fully. I'm suspicious when people tell me about friends they have who feel jealous of them because they lost weight, are getting married, taking a fabulous trip or got a promotion. If they aren't happy for you THEY AREN'T YOUR FRIENDS!

Your small and mighty group is more than a collection of people you like and share the occasional lunch with if you have nothing better to do on a Tuesday. They're people who love you. I believe fiercely in the power of community and family. I know that you can make someone's life measurably better by helping him or her along in small ways.

If you choose your small and mighty group carefully, you'll have the luxury to fall apart, make mistakes and express all of your flaws and fragility without apology.

This is not to say that you should surround yourself with sycophants who never challenge you or call you to the carpet when you're making cringe worthy mistakes.

Your small and mighty group will also tell you when you're wrong and question your decision making capacity when you decide that dying your hair fire engine red with black stripes is a fantastic way to celebrate turning forty. I deeply value honesty. I think that if your friends aren't going to tell you that your ass looks too big in those jeans, you need a breath mint, and you might want to grow a backbone, then no one will. If you're only going to surround yourself with people who tell you what you want to hear, you'll never grow or reach your full potential.

My friend Carolyn has triumphantly redefined herself. She went through a divorce, some tough child rearing years, even tougher career disappointments, and numerous moves searching for herself and her purpose. I'm fiercely proud of her. She has secured a great job, lost weight and is very happy with the life she's created for herself. Our friendship developed rapidly when she was in the early stages of what would become a major financial struggle and I invited her to move in with me knowing that she was in a dangerous financial position.

During that time Carolyn would ask for job advice, man advice, friend and parenting advice, and any guidance she could get because her internal compass was spinning and she found herself lost a lot of the time. What made me know with absolute certainty that Carolyn would find her true north and navigate her way to a better place was that she really wanted to hear the truth and she listened. Being better was more important to her than her ego. She listened to constructive criticism from her managers at work and her friends. She took good criticism like the gift that it is and she went and rebuilt her life.

Carolyn has been a sincerely loyal and committed friend to me. Like all of the members of my small and mighty group, she knows the best and the worst of me. She's been honest with me about my own life and it's the sort of reciprocity that I deeply value.

Without the extraordinary support of my remarkable friends I would not be in the place I am today. I couldn't have gotten here without these people. I don't know who I would be or where I would be without my friends, but I know that I wouldn't be here.

I've chosen people who contribute to the quality of my life and make me a better person, a better mother, and a better professional. Friendship is a decision. Decide that you're worthy of magnificent people and be a good and loyal friend. In the end relationships are all that matter in the world.

As you create your best life you'll be required to rely on your small and mighty group. Lean on them and know that relationships are dependent upon reciprocity. Be the friend that you deserve and give more than you take. Don't accept less. As I remind my students, if you expect nothing in life, don't be surprised when you get it.

Let go of people who don't contribute to your life and make room for those who will. I've cultivated my friendships. They're not accidental. I want people in my life whom I admire and inspire me to be my best self.

CHAPTER SIX

Change

"Change is inevitable - except from a vending machine."

ROBERT C. GALLAGHER

I f there's one thing that you can be certain of in life, it's that nothing will ever be static and remain the same. Change is constant. There are big changes that can alter the course of your personal life like death, the birth of a child, marriage, divorce, illness or job status. There are changes that impact our daily lives along with the course of history like changes in science, technology, politics, the economy, natural disasters and tragic events. And if all of that isn't enough change for you, there are fashion, nutrition, financial, and entertainment trends that change faster than we can sometimes keep up with. With all this constant change you'd think that human beings would be comfortable with change and embrace change as a condition of the human experience.

You only need to see one woman with electric blue eye shadow and the same beehive she's been sporting since before I was even alive to know that change can be hard. There's comfort in the familiar, which is why some men are still wearing a handle bar mustache long after the West was won. Change seems to imply a small death or loss of some sort.

If you want to build a life of your choosing you have to get comfortable with change. As the old saying goes, the landscape only changes when you're leading the pack, from the back it all looks the same. People get stuck with hair that should have gone the way of the dinosaur and jobs they should have quit a decade ago. It's easier to do what you know, than risk doing something new. Change for most people implies some risk or loss.

It's perfectly fine to have a job for thirty years if you love it, and if you like eating the same thing for lunch every day, and you feel that your leisure suit from 1972 is perfectly serviceable, that's okay too. But life is rich and expansive, so why on earth would you want to limit your experiences?

Research has proven that just by doing simple tasks a little differently, you can strengthen your brain and potentially stave off some forms of dementia. Think about that! Just by moving in a different way through life you have the potential to increase the strength of your brain.

I believe that, as Charles Darwin once said, "It is not the strongest or smartest that survive, but the one most adaptable to change."[10] This statement suggests a truth deeper and greater than ourselves. It expresses a truth residing in our genetic code that bears the weight of biology and evolution. A failure to adapt can mean death, ruination, or even extinction.

We're all at the mercy of external changes beyond our control, but there are also possibilities to create your own change. You have the power at any point in your life to reinvent yourself. You can decide to be different.

---

10 Charles Darwin, "Charles Darwin Quotes," Retrieved on November 23, 2012, Thinkexist.com, http://thinkexist.com/quotes/charles_darwin/

I often wear red lipstick or a pair of shoes so scandalous I could incur a fine. Women will walk up to me and whisper, "I wish I could wear that" or "I love that color, but I could never get away with it." What? Of course you can wear it; there's no law against looking fabulous. What do they think will happen to them? What do you think will happen to you if you wear vampire red lipstick instead of your usual carnation pink?

If you're in love with an electric orange rain slicker then wear it! Dance like a fool if you love to dance. Order breakfast for dinner and all side dishes for lunch if that's what you really want. Don't limit your options in life because you might disappoint your dead grandmother or you're worried that someone might not approve. Inhabit your body and the clothes you wear and the life you live. It's all YOURS and the precious time we have on this planet can be brief.

If it hadn't been for a major change in my life, I would most likely not be writing this book. Losing my job was a life altering change beyond my control. I didn't choose, wish or ask to be in the unemployed position I found myself in, but the change was an opportunity for me to live a larger, more fulfilling life. The change came during an inopportune time – a devastating economic downturn, but in all of that change and loss I have built my dream.

Change can be attached to loss, discomfort, and even pain, but it can also be liberating, exciting, and ultimately joyous. If you're in the darkest phase of your life, the great news is that it will change. Knowing that can buoy you. The ability to approach change with less resistance and judgment, and more excitement will strengthen your capacity to live more expansively.

Every year I make a decision to do something that forces me to stretch. It's not always within the context of my business, but I choose a project every year that will challenge my business acumen as well. In 2010 I set out to launch the Institute for Sales and Business Development. This year I'm doing a number of projects that are requiring new muscles and skills: scaling my business, expanding programs to new markets and writing my book, but this year I have also decided to grow outside of my business as well.

I started with organic gardening. Understand that my knowledge of organic gardening can be contained in the brain of an aphid, but I wasn't going to let that stop me! It's hard work, and there's A LOT to know. I have a very large plot and it took a great deal of heavy labor to prepare my little patch of earth to plant – although my friends have been great supporters and contributed hours of their time to help. Gratification is slow.

Early on, earwigs ate a lot of my meager crop; and my first attempt to lure them into death traps was a failure. I carefully followed the instructions of message boards and my master gardener who insisted damp rolled up newspaper and toilet paper rolls was like earwig Las Vegas, and for sure they would populate the dank tunnels, which I could then just collect and toss in the morning. But alas, my evil relocation project was thwarted, and now I'm on to diatomaceous earth.

From what I understand, insects cannot become immune and will die a painful death within 48 hours of contact or ingestion. This pleases me. I have gleefully dusted my entire garden with the powder.

I'm also going to be getting hens to lay fresh eggs, which I also know nothing about, other than sprinkling diatomaceous earth in the bottom of their coop can prevent them from getting mites.

But what does any of this have to do with my business? Gardening is far outside of my comfort zone. It's overwhelming and sometimes infuriating and frequently exhausting, but it forces me to find solutions to problems that seem insurmountable, and to devour information to advance my knowledge. I'm learning to be patient with myself and take pride in small victories. In business, problems no bigger than an earwig can devour your success if you aren't careful. It takes time, patience, and a willingness to get a little dirty to fix what's eating you or your business. It's not glamorous work and sometimes leaves you feeling defeated.

Pushing myself outside of my comfort zone has also given me a new level of empathy for my clients and students. I've always understood that asking them to prospect, ask for business or address objections can be daunting, but now I have a more nuanced understanding of how these small tasks feel more like battling giants than earwigs. My awareness doesn't make me less of a taskmaster, but perhaps I'm a more compassionate advisor and teacher.

Today make a decision to grow. Do something that scares you or feels too big. Go and learn to tap dance, learn to make a hat or surf. Do something that would surprise the people who know you or even better – yourself. I promise you'll learn something about who you are from putting on a pair of roller skates, building a piece of furniture, or learning to speak Italian.

Think about your own relationship with change. Has it hindered you or helped you along? Ask yourself:

- Do I avoid or embrace change?
- What was the last change I made in my life?
- Have I ever avoided a change that limited opportunity?
- Am I fearful by the idea of change?
- When was the last time I tried something new?

Most change doesn't kill you, except for the kind that does and there's not a lot that any of us can do about that! Why not change our relationship to change and rethink what might be possible? If you actually had the power to perceive something differently, anything might be possible.

CHAPTER SEVEN

Perspective

"Some people see the glass half full. Others see it half empty.
I see a glass that's twice as big as it needs to be."

GEORGE CARLIN

L ike most people who breathe oxygen, require food and water to survive, and occupy planet Earth, I have made some mistakes in the course of my life. Some of my missteps have been harmless and others have been more serious; all of them have been a result of being mortal, and none of them have killed anyone. This whole human thing is a fragile business. We all show up with our own stuff and do our best to behave like decent human beings and live as our best and highest selves. A lot of the time, probably most of the time, we do all right, and other times we blow it and make a bit of a mess. The best any of us can do at any given time is to acknowledge our failures, own our mistakes, and be better next time. That's it.

It took me a long time to figure this little formula out. I'm a little slow so I spent a lot of years battering myself over my mistakes. It didn't matter much if it was a typo in an e-mail blast or losing my patience with my children and raising my voice, I was determined to view these things as expressions of my character. I don't know why I attached so much power and significance to my failures, but it was a colossal waste of time and energy that didn't really serve any purpose other than to make me feel bad about myself.

Imperfection is very much part of the human experience. If you can learn to make room for flawed moments and lapses in judgment, you'll be a lot more productive and probably a hell of a lot happier. We're all vulnerable to error and imperfection at times, but those moments aren't necessarily who we are in total.

I'm a much more mature professional – time and experience have been excellent teachers. I strive for excellence, but now when I make a mistake I'm more analytical than emotional. Do a little post mortem of a deal you lost or a presentation you botched and evaluate what you could have done differently. It's behind you, but it can inform your future performance. Use your mistakes; they're rich with possibility and potential for greatness. I encounter people who behave as if their misstep is irrevocably damaging. People overcome mistakes. The world will forgive you, but if you want true meaningful change in your life, you have to forgive yourself.

I had a boss when I was working in real estate who laughed at his mistakes no matter how large. He was so focused on all of his success; he really didn't pay attention to much else. At one point when I worked for him I made a mistake which I spent the day apologizing for, analyzing, and beating myself up over. He became completely frustrated with me by the day's end, "Ann marie, that is ENOUGH!" He practically shouted at me in front of the entire team. "I cannot listen to one more word of this. You're smart. You made one mistake that no one but you really cares about, and you're wasting time and money talking about this stupid error and boring the hell out of everyone around you. I never want to hear about this again, never!"

I wanted to respond, but he made if very clear that he wasn't inviting a dialogue. What he said to me was true and taught me a lot about perspective and why I needed to get myself some. Shifting my focus didn't come easily or quickly, but it came and now perspective is a thing I very much value.

I want to be exceptionally clear: none of this is an excuse for bad behavior, unethical actions, or downright meanness – those things are of a different category and are not acceptable. I'm talking about just being human.

Obsessing over your errors and flaws is not healthy nor is it productive. It impedes your ability to learn and grow. People become so fixed on everything they don't have, can't do or did wrong. It's a truly horrible way to live and in no way contributes to success. There's a lot that's going to go wrong in life. Some of it will be your fault and much of it will be totally beyond your control and almost none of it will be life threatening. Whatever happens to you along the way, you get to decide how to feel and respond. Perspective is a rare and extraordinary tool. We all become so consumed with our own lives that we fail to see what's good and right. The next time you get a parking ticket, send out the wrong proposal, lose your keys, raise your voice, gain ten pounds or make a really bad decision – ask yourself how much this will matter in 1 week, 1 month or 1 year? Many things don't even matter much in a day or an hour, and yet we lose precious moments of our lives lamenting over small disappointments in the larger scheme of things.

I didn't really learn how to have perspective until my late thirties – my very late thirties. I'm not just speaking of optimism or magical thinking that everything will just work itself out, which can be a dangerous thing when used as a life strategy – that's just foolish. Perspective is an extraordinary gift that you give yourself. It's like purchasing more time in life because you stop wasting energy on things that matter very little and you start expanding the opportunities for growth, joy, celebration, and peace.

I've watched people waste years of their lives lamenting a decision, pining for the end of horrible relationship, or beating themselves up for some minor failure. It's wasteful and sad. When I finally realized that a deal I lost was not the last deal in the world, a poor parenting moment didn't define my whole relationship with my children, and the five pounds I gained could become the five pounds I lost, I not only had a lot more joy and peace in my life, but I was more successful personally and professionally. I was more directed and focused toward meaningful activity rather than being mired in meaningless negativity.

This isn't to suggest that my life is a musical and I break into song and overcome every challenge with grace. I have my moments, but they're infrequent, less intense, and brief. If you find yourself with a little pocket change, buy yourself some perspective. It's a gift that keeps on giving.

CHAPTER EIGHT

Your Decadent Dream

"Don't live down to expectations. Go out there and do something remarkable."

WENDY WASSERSTEIN

I must confess that I've always known what I wanted. What I want changes, expands and contracts over time, but I've never been confused about my desires. In the process of helping people realize their dreams, I've learned that many people haven't the slightest idea what they want. This was a great shock to me when I began my career as a coach and speaker. I would challenge people to articulate their decadent dream, the vision of the life that they fantasize about while they're drinking morning coffee, or commuting to work, the life they wish they had, but had no idea how to get. I thought helping people realize their decadent dream would be my work. I did a workshop with a friend of mine in which we told people to write down their decadent dream on a small piece of paper. We then read every dream as if we were liberating a pent up desire and offering it a chance for expression.

As we each read some of the slips of paper, I became stunned and saddened by how small and quiet some of the dreams were: I would like to lose twenty pounds, get out of debt, get a boyfriend. There was no imagination, no passion, or grand vision. This was supposed to be your BIG (all caps) unrealized dream. These are perfectly reasonable goals, but they're not and should not be your decadent dream. This compelled me to evaluate my approach to the idea of a decadent dream and think about helping people first to identify their dream.

I suspect that people really do have a decadent dream buried inside of them. I'm certain of it in fact, but I think that they don't have the skills or courage to say it out loud. Culture or family or experience has taught some of us that wanting something more than a mortgage, good health, and an occasional vacation is greedy or ridiculous. While I believe that we should be grateful for all that we have, I don't think we should punish ourselves for wanting more. Wanting to reach beyond the life you have doesn't make you ungrateful for the life you're currently living.

If you've never indulged in imagining a life that enables you to express your greatest passions and live fully, it feels scary or impossible or even ridiculous. You're very likely hearing every person who ever told you to be "responsible" or "sensible." Interestingly enough, I think making money doing what you love is quite sensible; it's simply not ordinary or usual. It's also coveted and seems reserved for the privileged few, a thing that is gifted, inherited, or a result of mysterious good luck. I don't put a lot of stock in luck. I believe that luck is created and decadent dreams are executed by a passionate, disciplined bunch, brave enough to venture down less worn paths.

The business of defining and articulating your heart's passion is nothing less than an act of courage. To examine your heart, your behavior and your own agency in the life you live at present, and the one you most want to live requires strength; and what if you tell the world what you want? The stakes are even higher and more frightening. You're exposing yourself to judgment and practically inviting unwanted commentary – right? Perhaps. Except, I think if you're quiet, apologetic, and fearful of your decadent dream, you have very little chance of realizing your own exceptional possibility.

When you identify and articulate your big ideas you give them power and voice. You claim your entitlement to fully inhabit your life and announce to the world that you are a force with which to reckon. But how do you even know what you want? How do you begin to ignite your imagination and envision who you might be?

As I have confessed, knowing what I want has never been my challenge, but having clients who are swimming in uncertainty and overwhelmed by possibility has required me to create tools to help them access their inner giant.

Seeing opportunity is not merely about having a positive attitude, it's about the capacity to imagine. It seems as though in our daily encounters imagination is exceptionally undervalued. There are simply not enough expansive, imaginative game changers who create their own opportunities and demonstrate to all of us, that there's extraordinary possibility outside of the bounds of our established thinking.

Think of Warren Buffet, Coco Chanel, J.K. Rowling or Steve Jobs. There's a superhuman drive that accompanies daring imagination that challenges our ideas about what is possible. Regardless of what you may feel or think about the short list of names I've mentioned, the truth is that each in their own right have or had infinite imagination and a mad love affair with the impossible, and each of them categorically rejected mediocrity or some lesser version of their vision. Let me be clear, these people are also highly disciplined, talented people who have the intellectual acumen to realize their vision. Imagination alone will not bring you wealth and success.

There are a couple of problems with imagination. First, it appears, or we believe that it's a gift rather than something we can cultivate, and secondly, imagination as an important tool for business seems almost laughable. If you can't teach imaginative thinking and the very idea is relegated to the category of soft and squishy, how do you ignite and commit to your imagination?

Imagination should be a goal of business and a way of life. The ability to reach beyond ourselves and explore uncharted territory is where the greatest opportunity resides.

Challenging our preconceived notions about how to earn, save, and grow money is critical in this ever changing and uncertain climate. Surround yourself with big thinkers who stimulate your creativity, inspire you, and challenge you. Thinking big isn't enough. You have to be a person of action. Surround yourselves with doers who aren't concerned about disturbing common beliefs. If there's something you don't know – go and learn it. If there's something you want to do, go and make it happen. Be your own champion and astonish yourself!

I took my boys on a vacation to Hawaii. We went with another family. We all decided we would do a full day excursion that would allow us to kayak, hike, zip line, and rope swing into beautiful swimming holes. This was the highlight of our trip. We were in one of the most beautiful settings in the world, creating this incredible experience with our children, and I was terrified. I'm deathly afraid of heights. A fear of heights is primal and resides in your body defying logic. While I have no problem flying all over the world in planes of all sizes, anything that involves looking over a ledge is paralyzing to me. My fear has become more pronounced as I've gotten older. I can't even ride a Ferris wheel. My knees weaken and move towards the earth. I sweat and feel a tremor from my head down to my toes.

When we came to the zip line portion of the excursion, they asked that everyone who felt they might not be able to do it, to please go first, because they would have to drive us back. There were only two scaredy cats in the bunch, and I was one of them. The other scaredy cat went first. I felt her fear and could see it emanating from every pore in her body. My voice cracked when I yelled up my encouragement to her. I took a deep breath in when I watched her jump off the platform, and my stomach fell just witnessing her colossal effort.

My two boys kissed me before I climbed the platform and everyone was clapping telling me that I could do it. I was just grateful to be wearing my sunglasses, because little did everyone know that my eyes were welling up with tears because I was so worried that I wouldn't be able to jump. This failure in my character made me feel fragile and weirdly vulnerable – things that I loathe feeling and exposing.

When I got to the top a girl young enough to be my daughter, leaned in to me and said, "You're going to be okay." I nodded silently. "Your boys are looking up at you right now and you're going to jump and they're going to be so proud of you!" I was fighting back tears because I could hear them below shouting, "We love you, Chicarita!" She finished clipping me to the line and said, "I'm going to count you down and then you're going to step off and fly. You just have to make me one promise, okay? I want you to keep your eyes open the whole way, it's so beautiful and I don't want you to miss a second." That young girl was doing what she passionately loved, she was having fun, and she actually was making a difference. Not a bad way to live your life.

When I have clients who are miserable in their current job or have a passion for something that they don't think can be monetized I have them ask critical questions of themselves to help shape what they might want to do and to help get at the truth of their decadent dream. I'm much more interested in helping people create a life rather than merely make a living.

Are you currently earning a living doing what you truly love? If you're currently earning a living doing what you truly love, then you're a rare minority and you should celebrate your good fortune. If you aren't then you're not alone. Many people aren't excited about their work, so many in fact that we all believe that there are no other options. I recently spoke to an attorney who proudly told me that he has worked in a job for a decade that he didn't like, but he's now making the money he deserves. Perhaps you might think it's admirable to suffer through a decade for more money, but that's not a decadent dream realized, but rather a prize for endurance. Every day some bold character decides that the path of endurance is not the path he or she wishes to take and tears off to leave a trail. If you answer 'no' to this question, just understand that you're making a choice to live as others have and there are other choices you can make.

What do you feel is your greatest talent or skill? This is often difficult for people to answer because we're trained to be modest. I'm an excellent speaker and superb with language. This might sound arrogant, but rest assured I don't print this on marketing material nor do I say this to anyone so plainly, but you need to be able to say it to yourself and yes, to others in an elegant fashion. I'm financially rewarded for my talents and skills. No one in their right mind would pay me to balance their financials or design a software system, but they do pay me to fly across the country and speak on topics in my area of expertise. Get comfortable with articulating your talent and embracing what sets you apart from others. You can't live your decadent dream if you're hiding yourself from the world.

What's the highest compliment someone has paid you about your talent or gift? This might seem an odd question, but it's designed with great intention. We've all been paid a compliment that makes us feel extraordinary and feeds us in a way that little else can. Recognition is significant and it's so much more than inflating our ego. When someone takes the time to compliment you, they're essentially affirming and validating your talent and skills, something you may not have been able to do yourself. Write down the compliment and consider how it made you feel. Are you getting paid to use your talents or are you dismissing those compliments as insignificant?

What part of your work or work you have done in the past, gives you the most pleasure? I love speaking, writing, teaching, helping people, creating new things, and coaching. When I started to build my company I wrote a list of things I really love doing and that I'm also skilled at doing, and then I found ways to monetize my talents. Sounds too easy? When you know how to create opportunities it's a lot easier than you think, but you have to begin with knowing what your sweet spot is and what gives you joy. There's a misguided belief that no one loves working and in order to make a good living you're going to have to do things you hate. This is a load of rubbish. I am proof that it can be different.

How much money do you truly want or need to earn to live what you define as a "good" life? Everyone has a different number. What's your number? How much money do you need to earn to have the life you want to live? This is a very scary thing for people to express and arguably this question is one of the more difficult on the list because we don't talk about money in our culture and we certainly don't go around saying how much we want to earn. We all work very hard and hope that we will work our way up a magical ladder and be rewarded enough money to afford us the life we desire. Is that your decadent dream? What is important to you that requires money? Is it a house, travel, your kids' education? Make a list of the cost of those things and how much you'll need to earn to have those things. This is important. You can't get to where you truly want to be without really knowing exactly where that is.

What do you daydream about doing? We all have moments when we're driving in the car or taking a shower and we imagine a life other than our own. When you think of that life, what are you doing that makes you so happy? We all have those yearnings, but most of us dismiss them as ridiculous or just pure fantasy. We feel foolish imagining some other existence so far from our own. I met a woman who runs a small boutique in Little Italy in San Diego. She sells clothing imported from France. In her small boutique she also has a space where she hand paints silk scarves and teaches others the art form. I engaged her in conversation and learned that she owns a home in the South of France where she invites students to come and learn how to paint on silk. She used to be a teacher, but she has completely redefined her life and earns a living in a completely unique and extraordinary way. She understood what she loved to do and created a business that would support her passion, talent, and lifestyle.

What would happen if you told the world what you really want to do? No one has actually died from telling the world his or her decadent dream. So why are we so fearful to tell people what we really want? I think we fear ridicule and failure. Every time I launch a project I tell the world what I'm doing. In part, because it makes me accountable, and also because they might be able to help me realize my vision by recognizing something I haven't even considered. If I'm just dreaming about an idea then it will never be born. Examine why you resist sharing your dream. What is keeping you from telling people? In order to fully realize your dreams, you need people to support you. They may be your family and friends. Hopefully they are, but if not, you need to create a support network that believes in you and supports your commitment to live your decadent dream.

Is the work you do now something you chose or something you fell into? It's not unusual for people to fall into careers that they didn't necessarily choose. It's possible to be quite competent and successful, but not feel as if this is your calling or your passion. I always ask clients how they landed in their profession, because I want to know if they landed there by accident or if this was a path of their choosing. Sometimes we fall prey to doing what is easy rather than what we wish. As I've said, living your decadent dream is an act of courage. It's also quite possible that you deliberately chose your business or profession, in which case you still must determine if the business continues to serve your interests and desires. It's okay to change your mind. I've known *many* professionals who chose to be teachers, accountants, attorneys and even doctors only to realize that they don't enjoy the work or the industry changed so drastically that the work is no longer what it once was. Give yourself permission to reinvent yourself. It's perfectly acceptable to decide that you want something else. The skills you've garnered in your profession will serve and inform your new venture, but it no longer has to be the focus of your work.

Do you know someone, or have you met someone who is earning a living doing what you would like to do? I ask this question of my clients for a couple of reasons. If you know of someone who is successful doing what you want to be doing, then first and foremost you know that it's possible. In addition, that person can be a valuable resource and wealth of information. It's been my experience that most people are willing to share their experience with you if you're gracious. There's no better education than the expertise of someone who has already done *it*, what ever *it* is that you want to do. By and large, people love sharing their wisdom and are flattered by those seeking direction. Even if you don't know someone personally and you've read a story about them online or in the paper, reach out to them and ask if you could have fifteen minutes of their time. You'd be surprised at how many people will say yes to you.

Do you look forward to your work? I can't tell you how many people I talk to who dread their work. We spend the vast majority of our lives engaged in work, not with family or pursuing our interests, but working. Why on earth would you commit yourself to a life of misery? I can say with absolute honesty that I'm excited by my work. This isn't to suggest that I love every minute of it or I don't have moments when I'm frustrated. It would be completely absurd and disingenuous to suggest that every detail of what I do is a joy. It's not. However, I wake up excited about working with my clients, speaking, training and writing. I love it and can't wait to begin my day. I love my work so much that it bleeds into my leisure time, not by necessity, but by choice. I write at the beach and on vacation, because my work is my passion. If you're turned on by what you do, you're in the right place. If you can't honestly say that you look forward to your work then you aren't living your decadent dream. If you're indifferent to your work then you aren't living your decadent dream and maybe indifference is satisfactory to you. That's perfectly fine if that's enough for you, but if it's not, just know that you can make another choice.

CHAPTER NINE

Trust Your Talent and Reach

*"Talent hits a target no one else can hit; genius
hits a target no one else can see."*

ARTHUR SCHOPENHAUER

I once heard someone say that he grew into every opportunity that he had been afforded. He was explaining that each opportunity is brand new and requires skills or experience that you don't necessarily yet have. I always appreciated this view, because too often, people focus on what they don't know, so much so that they fail to realize that there's so much that they do know.

I've taught a lot of people to position themselves as an expert. Here's the deal - you decide that you're an expert. There's no expert committee or expert certification or expert school that you can attend. Your collection of experiences, knowledge, and your unique point of view is what qualifies you to claim expertise. This can be an enormous challenge. You may grapple with feelings of inadequacy and cite everyone on the planet who knows more than you do, or feel fraudulent for claiming such a lofty title as expert. These feelings are real, but all they really do is degrade your ability to take risks and grow. They're ways of thinking that stop you from putting yourself out into the world for fear that you'll be exposed as inadequate.

There's no doubt that the higher the risk the higher the reward. This is just the basic math of living life on your own terms. I have a professional life that creates a lot of space for criticism. I teach and train people and am evaluated for my performance after every training, workshop, or class. I'm a speaker and writer and if all of that isn't enough, I perform in my own one-woman show, which creates a space for audience members and critics alike to criticize me for my writing or my acting or both! When it goes well, all of these things provide me a great deal of validation and acceptance, but I can't get there without risk.

You'll NEVER know everything there is to know about a particular subject and if you're constantly waiting to know more, you rob yourself of the experience and rewards of living your purpose and deny others the benefit of your expertise. You're effectively dismissing your gifts so that you can avoid any discomfort. This isn't a strategy for greatness.

Let me be perfectly clear. I don't advocate faking your expertise or lying. You shouldn't claim knowledge you don't have or take credit for work you haven't done; to do so is detrimental and only diminishes your integrity and value; but if you come from a place of integrity you have a right and duty to contribute your talent and intelligence to the world.

When I lived in Japan, I had the extraordinary opportunity to go to an International Woman's Conference. The experience was expansive and inspiring and 17 years later I still carry the lessons of the women who spoke at that conference. On one particular panel a Minister of Education from an African nation talked about crying in her office after she learned that she was elected. A colleague, a man, found her crying and asked what was wrong. She explained to him that she worried that she was not capable of this new, important role. He sharply explained to her that people who believed in her value were depending upon her and her anxiety was a luxury she could not indulge, because she owed it to those who supported her to inhabit the role she now possessed. He told her not to waste her time nursing feelings of inadequacy. He basically explained to her that she should never waste her time with such nonsense, because it took away from her service.

I've never forgotten that story and have tried hard to place my energy on delivering my best and highest self rather than diminishing myself. Imagine every first term President of the United States. How can anyone possibly be completely ready to be leader of the free world? At some point you inhabit the role and take it on where you are and you commit. Every President, CEO, performer, doctor, and attorney has had a "first," but there always has to be a "first" otherwise you'll never accomplish anything new or fulfill your highest purpose. A President will lead a country for the first time, a pilot will have to eventually take her first solo flight, a surgeon will have to cut open his first patient, and a child will take her first steps. You have to fully trust that your talent, knowledge, and skill will see you through.

I would never begin to suggest that you can eliminate your anxiety or discomfort. I don't believe that you can. I believe you have to live with that discomfort in order to achieve your highest self. Growth is born of discomfort. You simply can't learn to swim clutching on the edge of the pool. At some point you must push off and engage your whole mind and body. You may swallow some water or look a fool or embarrass yourself, but eventually you'll develop powerful muscles.

If you know that you avoid discomfort at all costs consider redefining your relationship with risk and try trusting your ability. It's a learned skill. At one time or another it's not unusual to fear that you'll be "found out." It's as if you've been a fraud all along and someone will pull the curtain back like the Wizard of Oz and discover that behind the booming voice there's nothing more than a small, scared man. Fearing fraudulence is a pretty common anxiety.

Lots of us at some point in time have crossed a finish line hoping that the accomplishment would make us worthy, only to realize that there were more finish lines we could run towards. If I win this case, if I land this client, if I close this deal, if I publish this article, if I get this speaking engagement, if I earn $1million, THEN I WILL HAVE MADE IT! If you have uttered any of these things or some version of them, you're not alone. Most of us have suffered from feelings of inadequacy at some juncture. There are always people more accomplished than us who might be smarter or more experienced and some how this compels us to diminish our worth.

The most glaring example of this for me came in graduate school when I conducted a pilot study for a social science class. It wasn't my field and I was anxious about doing well. I had turned in my study and presented, and the professor had asked if she could speak with me after class. I was married with a husband in law school and a newborn baby. Sleep depravation had become a way of life and showering was a luxury. I had no idea what my professor wanted to speak about, but I was pretty sure it might make me cry or quit graduate school. Sanity is difficult to maintain on 90 minutes of sleep a night.

My professor asked if I would be interested in expanding my study and publishing it with her. She told me that it demonstrated elegance in its simplicity and she thought it was worthy of greater exploration. I have no memory of how I responded. I went home and told my husband who was over the moon with excitement. While he was telling me how proud he was of me, I was feeling my feet tingle and my stomach contort with the realization that committing to publish would reveal my fraudulence.

I never answered my professor's calls or e-mails. I never published the study and I nursed that disappointment in myself for years. Upon the rare occasion that I've told this story, I generally get a response like, "Who are you talking about?" It seems inconceivable to those who know me well that I would surrender such an extraordinary opportunity and give into fear, but that is precisely what I did.

I can't retrieve that moment from my history. It marks a moment in time that fear was bigger than I was and it won. That doesn't happen to me anymore. I now create opportunities that scare the hell out of me and trust that I can rise to the occasion.

CHAPTER TEN

Success is Not Divine. It is Designed.

"Nothing will work unless you do."

Maya Angelou

I believe that you create your own luck and that success is not granted or gifted, but designed. This isn't to suggest that there's a grand plan with a set of directions; I promise you that you'll make lots of amendments, updates, and radical changes to your well-laid plans. Writers call it killing your babies. You may lovingly craft and nurture an idea only to discover that you must destroy it mercilessly. Remember this takes tough innards. (See Chapter One). It's the nature of bold designers of their own fate. You must be an agent of your success and engage in your vision with deliberate focus.

To design your success and your life is to honor your talent and ideas by committing to meaningful work and discipline. That's right, this is going to require some work. Anyone who tells you otherwise is a liar, liar pants on fire. When you meet people that appear to have sky rocketed to success or just got lucky, I strongly advise you to investigate that assumption. Odds are you'll find all the luck was created with a lot of heavy lifting and that comet-like ascension was more like pushing a boulder up hill.

Build discipline into your calendar like an appointment. What needs to occur to launch your business, write your novel or paint your masterpiece? Carve the time out and keep the appointment like religion. That's how it's done. This book is getting written not because I leap up every morning with the muse on my shoulder whispering what to write. The words are dutifully forming on the page, because I schedule my writing time and create page goals. For a long time I had 27 pages of this book. For months and months I had 27 pages. The book wasn't getting written not because I'm insanely busy, (and by the way I am). The book wasn't getting written, because I had no plan. I wrote when I felt like which turned out to be about a sentence or two every now again.

You may have a family and a job and feel that taking time to create your dream and personally enrich your life is both selfish and impossible. Both of those assumptions are a choice. You can decide that committing to your passion is a bold statement of self-love rather than a selfish pursuit and spending 15 minutes in the morning, 15 minutes in the evening and your lunch hour is better than no time at all. You decide.

When I started my company I was driven by necessity to earn a certain amount of money. I also made a decision about how much I wanted to earn and what I wanted to be worth, as well as the kind of work I wanted to do, what my personal life would look like, and when I wanted all of this to reasonably happen. Once I had this information, I was able to build a strategy and embed the activities that were necessary to execute my strategy into my daily life. Drafting goals is not a particularly sexy topic, but absolutely necessary to design your success.

I started by stating what I wanted: I want to launch my own sales and business development firm that provides sales training and coaching. What needs to occur for me to build this firm and what are both my input and output goals? The output goals state what I want and the input goals are a vehicle to get there. I love lists and crossing things off a list is as pleasurable to me as a walk on the beach – don't laugh, I adore nothing better than conquering something, even something small, that gets me to the next step of achieving my goal. It's more exhilarating than you might imagine.

Despite the fact that I do webinars, teleseminars, Skype interviews and engage with every social media tool under the sun, I really love paper and pen. A journal or notebook with a good pen are the first tools I reach for when building an empire.

I start by creating a list of what I want. I don't edit or judge, I just write it down. Once I have the list I start brainstorming all the things I need to do, who would be useful to contact, and from that list I create a set of goals that I want to accomplish within one week, one month, three months, six months, and a year. I craft my goals to be specific, measurable and realistic, but aggressive. Most importantly, I'm sure to create both input and output goals. When this is done I really have a plan to succeed. The plan doesn't in and of itself ensure success, but it's a necessary ingredient.

I also found that SWOT analysis was a great way for me to assess my position and approach my plan with a deeper understanding of my challenges and advantages. It's simple and yet efficient in design and deceptively basic, but provides clarity. SWOT is traditionally used as a marketing tool, but I've found it to be an excellent decision-making and strategy tool.

Here's a quick SWOT review that will allow you to use the tool for your own planning. SWOT stands for STRENGTHS, WEAKNESSES, OPPORTUNITIES and THREATS. STRENGTHS and WEAKNESSES are internal and things that you have control over while OPPORTUNITIES and THREATS are external factors you don't control such as the economy, trends in the market place, or your competition.

It's important when you write down your STRENGTHS and WEAKNESSES that you're brutally honest about both. Don't underplay your STRENGTHS and don't shrink from your

WEAKENESSES. The information is critical for you to accurately assess your position and decide how to leverage your exceptional talents and skills to craft an effective plan while providing you insight regarding where you're going to need additional training, resources, and support.

With OPPORTUNITIES and THREATS you want to be as expansive as possible. Think creatively about opportunities that others might not see and be as exhaustive as possible with your threats. Keep in mind that occasionally you may see an overlap. For my particular business, a challenging economy motivates people to pay for training and coaching, but budgets can be tight because there's resistance about spending money. This information helps me to leverage the economy as a motivator and address the spending objection up front with great confidence that this is the most important check they'll write for their business.

Once you have completely populated every sector of the grid you'll have a more clear perception of your position and how to proceed. As I've mentioned, I'm a list writer. So create your list, spread sheet or whatever tool that helps you form your plan into an actionable daily discipline, and VOILA! You are well on your way. I'm only sort of kidding here. It really takes less money and technology than you realize to launch a fabulous idea.

When I came up with my idea for The Millionaire Girls' Movement I was sitting at a Starbucks with my Marketing Director, Linh. Two weeks later I had a web presence as well as the logo, which is a photo of moi as the American icon Rosie the Riveter; and just two weeks after that I had secured interviews with international designer Zandra Rhodes and fitness guru Tamilee Webb. All I did was exactly what I've told you to do - nothing fancy. A lot of brainstorming, lists, input and output goals; add a cup of passion, a vat of enthusiasm and some work and poof, SHAZAM a movement is born.

If you're thinking that I have a staff or that this requires complete devotion, keep in mind that I did all of this while continuing to work in my company and do all the duties of single motherhood which include, but are not limited to, dental appointments, orthodontist appointments, fencing practice, football camp, beach trips, oil changes, bill paying, hair cuts, grocery shopping, vet appointments, gift buying, and, and, and…

While I get a lot of help from my mother who lives in a cottage behind my home, I don't have hired help of any kind. I do this in small incremental bite size bits until I've devoured a task. If you want something, really want it, you can have it if you know how to do what is required and are willing to do it. Those two criteria appear quite simple on the surface, which they are, but that does not mean it's easy.

Let me also confess that if I didn't have my mom doing the laundry, I would be wearing bikini bottoms for underwear or no underwear half the time. There are times when the same coffee cup is rolling around in the back seat of my car for weeks, because I don't have the five seconds or the brain power to take it out of the car. And I've gone two and half years at one point between dental appointments because getting my teeth cleaned seemed like an extravagance. So please don't think that I live some glamorous, exceptionally organized life. It can be stressful and at times chaotic, but it's never boring and more importantly it's very much a life of my choosing and design; and all day and every day that beats the hell out of a life I might have fallen into or can't escape.

This all probably sounds terrifically simple, maybe even too simple. The truth is most people agonize over doing something right. They agonize so much they never do anything. I once heard Joyce Carol Oates speak in Boston when I was in graduate school. Oates is astonishingly prolific and has written upwards of 50 novels and more than 30 short story collections. She also teaches. What a slacker! At the lecture I raised my hand and asked her how she managed to produce such a vast body of work. Oates replied that she felt as if she really "eked" it out. There was no magic. She explained her disciplined writing scheduled and how she integrated life with her husband and teaching. It sounded very sane and ordinary.

Doing is not all that magical, but it can be quite challenging. I like to say that just because something is simple doesn't mean that it's easy. Generally what keeps people from action is something going on in their head. Designing your ideal life and business is rooted in action that might be organized and deliberate or messy, but it's always action. I'm asked on a weekly if not daily basis how I manage to do everything that I'm doing. I work hard, *but* I also go to the gym with my son, walk my dogs, taxi my kids around and go to the spa once a month and yes I do occasionally sleep. The secret is, like Oates, I eke it out. I wake up everyday and engage in meaningful action to move my projects forward. You can be incredibly busy and never get anything done. I avoid tasks that fill time and focus on action that builds momentum.

Oh and don't forget to breathe.

CHAPTER ELEVEN

Accepting Failure, Criticism, and Compliments With Grace

"It's a rare person who wants to hear what he doesn't want to hear."

Dick Cavet

No one wants to fail or enjoys failing. If you're made of flesh and blood then criticism, even when well intended, and gently delivered, can sting. Experiencing failure and being criticized are evidence that you're engaged in life and put yourself out into the world. To be a creative force in the world is to understand that the extraordinary moments of euphoric success will be built on failures small and large. No one sets out to fail or misstep, it's merely an inevitable occupational hazard.

The good news is while failure isn't always fun, it can be filled with invaluable lessons that will inform your success, and if you can laugh at yourself and avoid beating yourself up, it can be a good excuse for a big glass of wine and a moment of reflection.

I've never, and I mean never, encountered an entrepreneur who hasn't felt the ache of failure, nor have I met a professional who hasn't had a moment they wish they could retrieve and burn in a beach bonfire.

When I was building my business, some endeavors lost money. Some ideas died on the vine and others inched towards a sad, slow death. At one point I wanted to produce a really high quality and beneficial self-publishing conference for writers. I thought it was an excellent idea, but it required more oversight than I had time to provide, needed a larger marketing budget, and more attention. I had some heavy hitting speakers, a spectacular venue and a great concept, but there were lots of structural issues. I lost time and money and made an executive decision not to lower ticket prices just to protect my ego. Lots of people thought that I should, but I knew better than that and I'm very glad that I made the decision to pull the plug. Fortunately for me, I was at a point professionally where I didn't feel that it was a failure at all. It was really a lesson in strategic planning. I made some bad decisions and didn't trust my gut a couple of times when I should have been more aggressive about commitments.

In the midst of the slow death of this conference, I heard an interview on NPR with the founder of PayPal who talked about how three or four business that he launched were failures to varying degrees before he finally launched Paypal. He was humble and self-effacing and honest and I thought: I am certainly not smarter or more skilled than this guy so if he learned from his failure and kept going than I can too. It was heartening and liberating to examine my choices with greater analysis and less emotion.

Once I clicked my lens and saw my mistakes as an education I was able to shrug off the loss and move on to my next endeavor. One of the reasons I'm so passionate about The Millionaire Girls' Movement is that women get to learn about the successes and the struggles around building your own wealth. If you give up after one or two failures, you may as well never bother entering the game.

Criticism is another unlikely gift if you're willing and able to receive it as such. I want to make one important point here, there are people who will criticize you for sport or to elevate themselves – generally this isn't the kind of critique that will serve you. Become adept at identifying those sorts of people and learn to shrug off what they say to you. On the other hand real, honest, quality criticism is a gift. I mention this in the chapter on Asking, but it arrives in this chapter as well, because too often I see people become defensive, hostile and shut down by good, honest feedback. You're going nowhere my friend, if you don't learn to really listen when someone has information that can make you a better professional or a better person.

The ability to receive criticism like a gift is a critical skill for success and one that most of us must develop. I did a presentation for Vistage and the Chair of the group said, "Once I started receiving criticism like a gift, it changed every relationship I had - including my marriage. When my wife expresses her frustration or disappointment, I say thank you for the feedback." It sounds sort of funny and pretty damned hard to do, but for the hell of it, try it for a week or two and see how it changes your life. In an effort to reframe how you receive criticism, consider the following:

Listen carefully before you respond. Most of us have a visceral response to criticism, because our perception is that it's negative. If we see the feedback as a positive contribution to our success, we're more likely to receive the information in a rational way. Take in the information and resist reacting. It's not easy to do, but controlling your initial response will serve you well.

Is the person providing the criticism experienced and a valuable asset to you? If the person who offers you insight is someone who has an opinion about everything and experience and knowledge about nothing then feel free to smile politely and disregard every word they utter. However, if the person who shares their insight is highly qualified and you know them as a reputable resource, then take what they're offering with gratitude, because it truly is a gift.

Have you heard the criticism before by someone else? If you've been given feedback on the same matter more than once, odds are there might be something to it and you should listen, even if the current person making the comment is a complete jackass. If a multitude of people in a variety of settings are making similar observations about you, it's either a remarkable coincidence or it's true. Now, you may have no interest in changing anything, but just understand that people are sharing an opinion of you that may serve you, and therefore it's wise to examine how important it is for you to remain the same.

Do you respect the person offering you feedback? You need to surround yourself with advisors who you respect and are courageous and invested enough to offer you insight. If the person who is critiquing you is someone you respect, his or her criticism is something you should also respect. I come from a theater and writing background where notes and critique are the primary vehicle for growth and education. You can't get better unless a director or teacher is telling you what's all wrong with your work. If you simply want to hear everything that's right with your work, you aren't going to grow. It's tough on the ego, but I've seen so many writers gravitate towards groups and classes that are non-critical, because they were terrified of anyone giving them honest feedback about their work. That's fine, but you aren't going to produce your best work if you aren't willing to improve on your weaknesses. Despite what many may think, acting and writing are hard work that require emotional strength. You need good people to challenge your work.

Be gracious and thank the person for having the courage to offer you insight that will make you better. If you want high quality feedback that will improve the quality of your work and advance your success, then seek out good feedback and be gracious when people provide you with that precious resource. Thank them. If you're someone who is fragile and defensive about your ideas or work, people will be reluctant to engage you and you'll compromise the quality of your work. Remove your ego and embrace criticism.

You should also learn how to elegantly and graciously accept a compliment. I haven't always done this myself. There have been times when someone paid me a compliment and I've shrugged it off, made a joke, or dismissed his or her assessment by somehow belittling myself. It's a terrible insult to someone who is giving you a gift. It's as if you're saying, "This gift is no good," You diminish yourself as well as the person complimenting you. When you graciously thank someone you return his or her generosity. Learn to receive a compliment. Smile and thank people. Tell them how much you appreciate their generosity.

I very much understand the compulsion to diminish or deflect compliments. I was well trained growing up and could deflect a compliment with more skill than the Karate Kid could defend a kick to the head. The training was detrimental. It may seem counterintuitive to embrace and receive compliments. It may even collide with your upbringing, which might have taught you that humble people and good girls don't accept compliments. I want to challenge you to rethink your reaction to compliments.

Compliments and criticism are strange sisters, but our relationship with both can inform the way we feel about ourselves; and how we proceed through life. If we can accept criticism and compliments with grace, we get to use criticism to our advantage, and enjoy the pleasure of a lovely compliment.

CHAPTER TWELVE

It's Okay to Cry

"Only a man who knows what it is like to be defeated can reach down to the bottom of his soul and come up with the extra ounce of power it takes to win when the match is even."

MUHAMMAD ALI

A mong those who know me well and those who barely know me, I'm perceived as a tough cookie. I write a lot about tough innards in this book, but we're all human and I think that it's both appropriate and correct to express your exhaustion, fear, or disappointment. Success is rarely a steady ascent. There are painful losses and unexpected disappointments along the way that challenge our commitment and impede our progress. I've had many of those moments and sometimes I cried.

This isn't really a chapter on crying. This is really about giving yourself the room and freedom to release your anger, disappointment, and sadness when things don't go your way, because sometimes they don't, and that moment is like a wave that crashes into you and knocks the breath right out of you. I've found accessing that space very difficult at times. It's not natural or easy for me to succumb to fragility, but I think it has an important place in the process of living my greatest life. That said, you need to have some control over your emotional expression.

I've encountered many women, very powerful women, who have confessed that they cried during a review or when they were criticized. It's an embarrassing moment. It's fair to say that most of the professional women I know would do nearly anything to avoid such a public display of vulnerability. It's important that you learn to control your emotions, lest they control you. That's precisely why I discuss so carefully how to manage criticism. You're going to get a review that you perceive as unfair, you'll be wrongly criticized at times, but your ability to approach that moment from a position of neutrality is imperative.

If you have no control over your response, you appear less powerful. I'm not suggesting that you don't ball your eyes out and scream into your pillow at times, but understand that as you shape your brand, it's important that you express confidence and power. Avoid being easily affected by others. None of us are perfect, but I strongly advise you to find a way to have critical conversations from an emotionally neutral position. It will serve you well and expand your options.

I once coached a young attorney to help her with her business development. She was a bright, strong, young woman who confessed that she had a tendency to react in a hostile way to colleagues who challenged her. She shared some scenarios with me and confessed that she knew this was hurting her career. She wasn't one to cry, but rather lash out aggressively if someone crossed her in any way.

We worked on finding what was triggering her reactions and then we built a strategy and set of rules for her to follow to mitigate her volatility. After a month of approaching critical conversations with more neutrality and thought, she was treated entirely differently by colleagues and partners and was afforded more opportunity. She learned that her power came from control and not from explosive behavior that may have intimidated people initially, but ultimately caused them to perceive her as out of control.

Here are some thoughts on how to manage critical conversations that might make you emotionally reactive.

Take one or two beats before you respond to something. Slow down the process and breathe. There are times when we're confronted with a situation that creates a visceral reaction. That funky feeling in your stomach, your tightened jaw, or your heart racing are indications that you are anxious, angry or upset and might say something that will be of disservice to you. It's deceptively simple, but incredibly effective. Slowing down your breathing can slow down your heart rate and your brain long enough to articulate a more reasonable response. Sometimes even taking a step back physically will literally put you in a different space and help you harness control.

Ask questions and validate that what you're "hearing" is accurate. Very often what we're hearing has absolutely nothing to do with the intention of the person speaking. I like to joke that sometimes not only are we not in the same movie we're in separate movie theaters miles apart. Always repeat what you think you're hearing so that you're operating from a place of mutual understanding. This is equally important when you're delivering feedback. Ask someone to repeat what they think you're saying.

When necessary, respectfully ask for some time to consider the person's perspective. Sometimes everyone is better off if you can take a bit of time to process a difficult moment. Respectfully ask someone if they wouldn't mind if you took a day or even two to process their position before you respond. This will allow you to create a space to think about what someone is really saying to you and decompress a bit. It's a valuable technique that can be the most effective path to a solution. I promise you that no quality discourse takes place in an anxious or reactive environment. One or two days can purchase a lot of clarity and positively impact the outcome of your communication.

Maintain a neutral tone even when you're angry. This isn't easy to do. Again, I recommend breathing. We all lose our patience with our children, our partners, our colleagues and even someone who provides poor service. When you raise your voice or allow someone to get a reaction from you, you're more likely to cry or yell or behave in a way that isn't becoming of a powerful, confident, professional.

Express your anger and disappointment outside of the moment. When you aren't in the moment I think it's important to vent and express any pent up hurt, anger, disappointment or even outrage if you're so inclined. Friends and family are important sounding boards. If you don't express your emotions away from the situation you risk reacting without control and dignity.

Authentic frustration should absolutely be expressed and released, but on your own terms. Don't be at the mercy of a visceral response that gets away from you. Give yourself permission to cry, yell, and break a dish or two, just make sure that it's a moment of your choosing.

CHAPTER THIRTEEN

Celebrate Along the Way

"Come quickly, I am tasting the stars!"

DOM PERIGNON

Don't wait to land your first large account or make your first million to celebrate. Part of maintaining your motivation and continuing to do what's required to live your decadent dream is to celebrate the small victories. Depending on the day, sometimes I celebrate that I wrote one page, sent an overdue invoice that had been hanging over my head or drafted a proposal. Now, I don't send myself to Paris or on a shopping trip to New York for these modest victories, but I might get a pedicure or buy myself a really nice candle or indulge in a good piece of chocolate or simply take time to walk on the beach. These small celebrations validate my work and inspire me to continue.

In truth, those small victories are meaningful and move you towards your bigger vision whatever that may be. I actually learned this from my clients who would get giddy from merely researching their idea. They would delight in small achievements and find joy in their work while I was waiting to make it across the finish line. Observing my clients taught me to see that the small successes were worthy of acknowledgement.

This might sound a little soft and fluffy – not the sort of thing you would expect me to bother talking about, but here's the thing - if you don't find places to lift a glass, give yourself a pat on the back or glory in your accomplishments, you're going to find it challenging to maintain your enthusiasm. And let's face it - waning passion is no condition to be remarkable.

I make an effort to keep a bottle of Veuve Cliqout in my refrigerator at all times. I advise my sons to do the same when they become of age because one never knows when there might be an opportunity to celebrate, and when that moment arises you want to be prepared to properly rejoice. Some of my fondest memories are small moments of triumph that were celebrated with no more than a friend or two with a bit of cheese and a bottle or two of wine. Beyond how this will contribute to your motivation, this is where life exists at its finest.

I regularly get e-mails from people who heard a webinar of mine, found The Millionaire Girls' Movement or heard me speak. The e-mails are generally expressions of gratitude for my work. They don't always lead to opportunity; they're merely people taking the time to let me know that my work matters to them. These are magnificent little victories that inspire me to stay the course. My work isn't merely how I earn my living, it's the mark I make on the world. When someone takes the time to express his or her appreciation, I take a moment to properly value the effort.

This is also about really taking enjoyment and pleasure in the process. Fun is good. When you have more fun you tend to be more successful or at least this is true for me. Misery and boredom are poor breeding grounds for success. You need light and air to expand.

CHAPTER FOURTEEN

Be an Excellent Boss to Yourself

*"By working faithfully eight hours a day you may eventually
get to be boss and work twelve hours a day."*

ROBERT FROST

Do you remember when you were young telling your playmates,
"You're not the boss of me?" Well, now you are the boss of you.
When you make a decision to create your own opportunities,
you're your own boss. This is one of the perks and the challenges
of living on your own terms. I haven't always been a great boss
to myself. Sometimes I'm a slave driver and I've been known to
be unforgiving about even the smallest failure. Although, I have
greatly improved on this matter (see Chapters 7 and 11). When
I'm hired as an Executive Coach, I often say that people pay me
to be their boss. Self-discipline is imperative to creating your own
opportunity, but it's also difficult.

As your own boss, you should set high standards for yourself if
you want to achieve your decadent dream. If you set a low bar, you'll

reach it every time, but you won't get the gold medal. I'm sorry to tell you that everyone is not a winner in this game, and it's up to you to be demanding of yourself. If self-discipline was a simple matter there would be no personal trainers, athletic coaches, singing coaches, executive coaches, etc…You're embarking on a journey that will require a great deal of yourself, but ultimately you're going to be the only one making such demands.

If I don't get out of bed every day and write this book it's not going to get written, but no one will care either. I'm accountable to no one other than myself. If I wanted to sleep half the day and watch daytime TV from my bed while eating banana cream pie, there would be no consequences other than the fact that I wouldn't earn any money and my body would expand. People who imagine that being their own boss will be this delicious reward might be disappointed by the reality. Even if you telecommute, you work for someone who requires you to produce. While working from home requires greater discipline than going into an office everyday, it certainly isn't the same as having to show up for yourself everyday.

Think about the kind of boss you want and the sort of boss you'll need. You want a boss who is respectful and supportive, but you'll require a boss who is demanding and pushes you to trust your talent and reach, and not get stuck by fear or be hampered by procrastination, and excuses. In order to get the best performance from yourself you need to be kind to yourself, demanding of yourself, and brutally honest.

I list kindness because it's easy to beat yourself up, which as it turns out, is a complete waste of time. When you're struggling, if you can find time to feel bad about yourself, then guess what? You can find time to focus on the challenge and get over the hurdle! Yes, the exclamation point is me raising my voice. Too often I encounter people who want to sit in their misery and express why they aren't smart enough, rich enough, thin enough, or what ever enough to get what they want. The years wasted on self-abuse aren't going to get you any closer to what you want. Step outside of yourself with the courage to be brutally honest about what's going on and you will already be one step closer. Honesty can come hard, but it need not be unkind.

I've learned from bosses of my past, some of whom were downright crazy, and others who understood the importance of mentorship and cultivation and have been great contributors to my success. I've worked very hard on being an excellent boss to myself, because if I have anything to do with it, I'm the one and only boss I'm ever going to have. I have a duty to develop myself as a good leader in my own life.

When you make the decision to create your own opportunities and build your own empire, you need to write a job description for the CEO of your little empire and then you'll need to assess whether you have the skills for that position and if you don't, how will you develop those skills?

The most common struggle an entrepreneur faces is the ability to generate revenue and create opportunities. The entrepreneur's ideas, products or service might be genius, but without the skills to monetize their work, they can't survive. Many entrepreneurs have approached me in my training sessions who truly never realized that their most critical skill would be sales and business development. It's an overwhelming realization that usually comes in the form of a lot of expensive pain of lost revenue. I'm completely serious when I tell you to draft a job description and determine if you have the necessary skills to blaze your own trail.

Being my own boss is one of my greatest professional joys. There is not a single thing I miss about working for someone, but it's critical to devote the requisite energy to professional development so that your self-leadership serves you at the highest level. Don't assume that you're a natural born self-leader. Assess what will be demanded of you and determine where your weaknesses are so that your organization, no matter how small or large, thrives under your leadership.

Self-knowledge is a difficult business that requires honesty, analysis, and an ability to step outside of one's self. These are not easy things. Some people are so self-critical that they can find nothing right about their work while others are so certain about their ability that they don't see opportunities to improve and grow. Both strategies compromise your success. Being overly critical of your work and shy about promoting your value doesn't serve you. Think about it. Would you want a boss who found everything wrong with your work and never praised you? Of course not! So don't be that sort of boss to yourself.

Take care of yourself. Women in particular still struggle mightily to think of themselves first, and I want to challenge you to consider where you place yourself on your list of priorities. Your position expresses your value both to yourself and the rest of the world. I recently spoke with a colleague who said that the quality of her life is being compromised by her inability to say, "no." This is common even among extremely successful women. I myself am learning to say "no," but more importantly, to say, "yes" to myself first.

You are your most valuable asset. Your children will thrive, your partner will benefit, and your professional life will flourish when you are your best and highest self. To be your best and highest self is to nurture you. Find sacred time that you protect for yourself even if it means saying "no." If you're someone who can't say, "no" start with, "let me think about it and get back to you." Depleting your most important asset is costly both personally and professionally. Your time has a value so understand that and make decisions with the knowledge that we're all allotted a finite number of hours and not a minute more. Just because you can do it all doesn't mean you need or should to do it all.

Dispense with guilt and find yourself at least one hour that's completely yours. Spend that hour on yourself any way that you choose. The value to your health, relationships and work is incalculable. View yourself as the priority. You can only give what you have, so if you're exhausted, overworked and fragile, that's what you're giving to your job, your children, and your partner.

Protecting your most important asset isn't something we generally discuss in any measurable way, but the truth is there's a real emotional and financial cost to depleting yourself.

No matter how much money you earn in your lifetime, you'll never be able to purchase more time, not ever. Spend your time wisely and judiciously and give yourself time.

CHAPTER FIFTEEN

Be Tenacious but Patient

*"Patience and tenacity are worth more than
twice their weight of cleverness."*

THOMAS HUXLEY

'm not known for great patience. Patience has been a virtue I have nurtured carefully and consciously. It's a particularly challenging trait when the wolf is beating at your door. Tenacity and patience are strange friends, but you desperately need both of them in equal measure to live a life of your choosing. When you're building something from nothing there will be moments when you want to simply fold, and what will get you to the other side is tenacity and patience.

Tenacity is the ability not to merely show up, but to keep showing up again and again and again and again, when others would have dropped out of the game long ago. It's that fifth call you make to a prospect that you make sound like it's the first contact, and the ability to redesign your product for the sixth time, because your initial attempt and the five attempts after that failed. It's the ability to send another article to a publisher after ten rejections. Tenacity is fed by passion and desire and it fuels your growth, there's no question of that, but without patience you might go a little crazy.

I have come to accept that when something is beyond my control, it's not going to happen fast enough for me. This acceptance hasn't come without great frustration along the way. Empire building is a constant process of reaching a new height only to realize that you're not quite there. Every cliché phrase you've ever heard about the "journey" is completely true. What appears to happen overnight takes much longer in reality. Phrases like "over night success" and "bursting on the scene" are so wildly inaccurate and such a disservice to those building something from nothing.

Take heart and learn from true empire builders. Steve Jobs lost a million dollars a year for something like five years when he first invested in Pixar. It took many years to perfect the science and develop the creative genius that would catapult the company to a giant in the film industry. There were many struggles within the business and the technology that created one obstacle after another. Thousands upon thousands of hours were committed to Pixar's success, although to the outside world it seems that Pixar launched with *Toy Story* and then made one hit after another in rapid succession.

Ellen DeGeneres thought her career was over and stopped working for many years before the revival of her career came with the *Ellen Show*. She has spoken openly about the crushing disappointment and long road back. It's rarely a clean and constant ascent to the top for anyone.

As I've mentioned before, Max Levchin, Paypal's co-founder had four failed businesses before the financial success of Paypal. Levchin said, "The very first company I started failed with a great bang. The second one failed a little bit less, but still failed. The third one, you know, properly failed, but it was kind of okay. I recovered quickly. Number four almost didn't fail. It still didn't really feel great, but it did okay. Number five was PayPal."[11]

---

11 Max Levchin, interview by Renee Montagne, National Public Radio, Silicon Valley, October 29, 2009

This year I'll be performing my one-woman show. The show started with one short story that I wrote six years earlier, a story that was rejected by more than one publication. In 2009, I spent some time in and out of a writer's read-and-critique group and finally in 2011 I went to Santa Fe to work with a woman named Tanya Taylor Rubinstein who would coach and mentor me through my first draft and production of *Renegade Princess*. I didn't know the twists and turns my writing would take, but I kept showing up and writing and editing and writing some more.

When I started interviewing successful women like Jenny Craig and Zandra Rhodes for the Millionaire Girls' Movement, I noted that they all said the same thing. You have to be patient about your business or ideas and then the money will come. Working endless hours, taking risks, making sacrifices and absorbing disappointment and failure has fueled my passion. Your love and passion for something, what ever that something is will inspire you to rise to every challenge, push yourself outside of your comfort zone, and create opportunity. Money alone won't sustain your drive.

We're all in love with success stories. We love the idea that people built something and were justly rewarded with wealth and recognition. But without the tenacity, resilience and patience to assume the risk, dedicated time and the rise up from failures, there would be no success stories to celebrate. The American dream has informed our belief that you can be and do anything no matter who you are or where you came from. That's the promise of American citizenship, and I still believe in that promise despite the political, economic and social struggles of my generation. I still believe that we live in the most remarkable country in the world rich with possibility.

The impact of global economic strife and uncertainty has certainly compromised our collective American optimism in possibility. We have become fearful and overwhelmed with obsessions of doom and despair. In fact, we're indeed in crisis, but I think we have a lot of choices around how we respond to this crisis. I have elected to pursue my decadent dream in the midst of a loud and ever increasing persistent voice that informs me on nearly a daily basis that there is no opportunity. The very notion of pursuing your decadent dream seems almost outrageous in a time when people express gratitude for poor paying, unfulfilling jobs that they hate, but I'm successfully managing this vast and uncertain terrain in defiance of all the negative noise telling me that it's not possible. It's not because I'm particularly special, but more because I'm tenacious and patient.

A job where someone pays you provides an alluring illusion of security and comfort, but with unemployment rates holding strong and companies cutting hours and benefits, my pursuit to earn a living doing what I love on my own terms feels much more empowering and dare I say – secure. I have no control over whether some company that employs me will fail or succeed, but I'm responsible for my own success, the quality of the work I put out into the world, and offering something of value to the marketplace.

I learned long ago that the difference between those living their decadent dream and those who aren't is *action*. This was confirmed for me every time I interviewed someone for The Millionaire Girls' Movement. Nearly every successful woman said that at some point you have to do something, even if you don't feel ready, even it you think it's not perfect. Your decadent dream is nothing more than fantasy wrapped in hope if you never act.

I grew up in a culture of poverty that only knows survival, but in college I learned what it meant to be from a culture of poverty and I made a conscious decision to live differently. It hasn't been easy to break away from the legacy of survival. When survival is what you know – survival is what you do. It's important to seek examples of people living their decadent dream. I like to tell people that I'm an excellent student of success. I pay attention to people who have created what I want.

I no longer want to merely earn a living. I want to leave a legacy. When I was in college I took a Cultural Anthropology class that was completely horrible. I love Anthropology, but the professor was a hot mess, utterly disorganized, and as exciting and engaging as a jar of paste. I only remember learning one thing in that class. That one lesson was worth every other painful moment and arguably may have been the most important realization I made about myself in college. It has informed my professional development and challenged me to redefine my future and the future of my children.

I learned about my culture: the culture of poverty. My mother was a single mother who worked hard at a pharmacy for more than twenty years, barely earning enough to sustain us. Let me be very clear. I'm not ashamed of that upbringing. My mother was a woman with a strong work ethic and I wouldn't be where I am without her. Her history is part of me and my success is a testament to her incredible love, support, and generosity. But what I learned from her was how to survive. That's what my mom knew how to do, and that's what she taught me. I didn't learn middle class skills of saving for a rainy day or the skills of the wealthy who pass down different lessons altogether, take different risks, and see opportunities that cannot be viewed when gripping a life preserver to keep from drowning.

I still remember reading about the culture of poverty, as if it was a prognosis of my financial future. It was comforting to understand that my decisions had been informed by years of training that didn't breed wealth, but it was terrifying to learn that I would have to overcome that training and write a new story.

Redefining my legacy is a conscious effort. I have moved outside of my culture. To transition out of a familiar culture requires consideration and yes, courage. I had to claim my piece of proverbial real estate in this new culture. I had to liberate myself from feelings of guilt about rejecting a culture that had taught me to survive, but kept me from becoming wealthy.

I invite you to rewrite your story and make the fearless move to earn your worth and build your own empire if that's what you truly desire. Owning your time, earning your worth, making a difference, and choosing how to make a living is powerful, but you'll never know just how powerful, until you begin.

BIBLIOGRAPHY

Dickenson, Emily. *The Complete Poems of Emily Dickinson (Variorum Edition)*. Ed. R.W. Franklin, Cambridge: Harvard University Press, 1999.

Dirks, Tim. "Filmsite Movie Review of the Wizard of Oz." Retrieved on December 31, 2012. http://www.filmsite.org/wiza5.html

Eliot, Thomas. "Prufrock, and Other Observations." Retrieved on December 31, 2012. http://www.bartleby.com/198/1.html

Frankl, Viktor. *Man's Search for Meaning.* Boston: Beacon Press, 2006.

Geisel, Theodor Seuss, *Oh the Places You'll Go,* New York: Random House, 1990.

Goodreads.com. "Coco Chanel Quotes." Goodreads.com. Retrieved on December 31, 2012. http://www.goodreads.com/author/quotes/3004479.Coco_Chanel

Goodreads.com. "Henry Ford Quotes." Goodreads.com. Retrieved on November 23, 2012. http://www.goodreads.com/author/quotes/203714.Henry_Ford

Lipman, Joanne. "The Mismeasure of Woman." *The New York Times,* October 24, 2009. New York edition.

Refspace.com "Warren Buffett Quotes." *Refspace.com.* Retrieved on November 23, 2012. http://refspace.com/quotes/Warren_Buffett/rich

ThinkExist.com. "Charles Darwin Quotes." *ThinkExist.com.* Retrieved on November 23, 2012. http://thinkexist.com/quotes/charles_darwin/

ThinkExist.com. "Percy Ross Quotes." *ThinkExist.com.* Retrieved November 23, 2012. http://thinkexist.com/quotes/percy_ross/